The Power of So

Kevin Carly

Dedication

For the citizens of the United States of America in 2024.

What do you really want to solve?

There is still time and hope.

Don't fuck it up.

Acknowledgment

I'm sure there are thousands of people I could acknowledge here and still miss thousands more. These lessons and the content that goes along with them were inspired by so many and may even be experiences munged together to make up one story I experienced with many different people.

What's important to me is that I thought of you, each of you, as I wrote this. Sometimes it brought tears to my eye. Tears of fond memories. Tears of love. Tears of knowing that next time I see you I may have to actually run really fast.

Yes, here and there I took some artistic license. But I did so out of love…the love of telling a good story, sometimes at your expense and getting a good laugh as many of you have known me to do so often.

So at the fear of forgetting anyone, please forgive me if I do, here we go. A huge hug and thank you to the following:

For Ilens Dort, for getting me on the path.

All the people who have inspired the lessons, real names or otherwise. The many Alices and Bobs mentioned herein. Likely you were mentioned because you might be missed. I'll work on my aim. Craig…Brown? My lifelong friend Brent Taylor for providing the basis for the first two lessons and being my lifelong friend. Kim Flagstad, for the German blueberries. Bill Jenks, the greatest all-time mentor.

My family, especially my children Nikolas, Zakory, Kaleb, Haillie, Abigail, and Brigham. Nonna and Nonno. My friends who I know are there if I need to call, Stevis Arnold, Deanis Chase, and

Jenny Caldwell. My old sister, Gena Bertelsen, for eating that dessert that spawned the one fib in this book. We all know you did. Vengeance is mine! For my brothers, Jeff and David, who will confirm my version of the dessert story. My new sister, Marti Beecroft, for being a freaking rockstar and doing that DNA test. For my mom, Geri, for being mom…and doing your DNA test just to be sure.

Thanks to the KDP Publishing team for helping me turn this into a reality!

My team members through the years, but especially the current one (and you know who you are, but Jake and Robert said named mentions will be cause for royalties. I disagree. Now I need to mention Adair, Alex, Bill, Brian, Cindy, Darren, Don, Dwight, and Ray, plus honorable mentions going to Audrey, Emily, Judy, Michelle, Natalia, Sandra, Taylor.) Praise the old gods, the new gods, all thc gods in between, we lifted each other up to new heights. And with each new team, those heights reached…heightier heights.

Finally, thanks to Jen Thayer for trading my Pokémon card to Daisy Seow. And thanks to Daisy for surprising me every weekend, for playing our games, and for saying exactly the right thing exactly when I needed to hear it to get me out of my rut and finish this book. The universe might just know what it's doing.

Preface

The Power of So has been years in the making. It started unknowingly when my dear friend, Brent Taylor, taught me and my best friend, David, the basis of the first two lessons, to do a good job and get paid.

Those lessons didn't have the steak behind the sizzle, so to speak. It was just great advice from a great man who was looking out for some young people. He had a lot of advice for us when we were searching for advice and guidance. We were sponges then.

As time passed and we began to fill our quivers with arrows, both David and I followed similar paths. Both of us found some amount of joy in technical careers.

Though we weaved back and forth, we found ourselves often working for the same employers. Sometimes we would drag along other great people with us, or they would drag us, like Stevis and Deanis, familiar names rather than their more appropriate family names.

I can confidently say the greatest moments of my early career, the most successful times, had some level of involvement with these three humans.

And yes, some of the worst times of my life were witnessed by them, too.

Yet some of these anecdotes may be very familiar to Stevis and Deanis. David…he hasn't returned any calls since he passed away a couple years ago. He was a master storyteller, and probably he would have insisted that if I'm writing a book about filters and problem solving, I would be best served by starting off with a chapter about the night the green hand of death woke up my mother.

He wouldn't be wrong. A good filter and some Pepto would have solved that problem. Maybe too little, too late, but he would have a point. I digress.

But these stories may be familiar to those who were involved, artistic license aside. After a while, the people who were involved started insisting that these stories, that had become rules and lessons, should be a book.

You see, with each team I led, I applied these rules and lessons to the way I taught and coached my teams. These are the ways I helped them understand how and why we solve problems.

Some people just aren't born to be problem solvers. Me, I hunt them down. I've hired biologists, archeologists, teachers, waitresses, retail workers, people buried in the wrong career. Maybe it's better to say they had not yet found their right career and helped them get into technology by starting them in technical support.

And then with the right guidance, some people can be turned into problem solvers extraordinaire. People who know how to ask the right questions, who can seek to focus upon what problem they are solving.

They are people who filter out the noise. They understand what it means to blueberry the shit out of a situation.

These lessons affect them at work, at home, everywhere.

And then one day, someone who used to work for me, Ilens Dort, asked me to meet up with him for breakfast. Right out of the blue. By the old gods and new, I think we hadn't spoken in perhaps a dozen years.

It was Ilens who put me up to the challenge and, quite frankly, I failed to meet that challenge.

I can provide all the reasons here. Covid19. A sudden onslaught of migraines that put me on a three-month medical leave. A car accident that resulted in a total hip replacement. Divorce. All of these are reasonable and justifiable interruptions. But in the end, my discussion and agreement with Ilens was about accountability.

I failed that test according to our agreement.

Nevertheless, I did persevere over time. As I suggest in the Service Over Resolution chapter, it's about the journey. And believe me, writing this book has been one helluva journey.

Once I got to the point where only three chapters remained, it was September 2023. I had writer's block. Several personal struggles not worth mentioning here were hounding my gray matter. The universe had cried out to me something I couldn't reconcile.

And my dear friend Brent was in horrific health.

I finally managed a drive out to his home in Colorado for a visit. With David's wife, Jenny, I was able to visit Brent.

It was wonderful to see him after so long. At the same time, his failing health was a reminder of my own mortality. I'm not getting younger. Part of my discussion with Ilens was my legacy and how this book was part of it.

I have to be honest in saying that I went into a bit of a depression. October passed, then November. With December, I faked a good smile all the way through Christmas.

I had a surgery scheduled to remove a Morton's neuroma from my left foot. Because that would interrupt my normal schedule, and I'm a bit OCD about my schedule, I had to stop into my regular weekend breakfast place.

This is where some more dear friends, Jen and Daisy, work and I visit there every weekend for breakfast. I've done this for the greater part of 20 years. I'm a creature of habit, you might say. Or as that Cheers song goes…well, anyway…

Daisy, the server to whom I am permanently assigned (long story…very long story…) is incredibly dear to me. She knew I was stuck in the book. She knew I was down a bit. As I was about to leave, Daisy gave me a bit of an amazing "Win one for the Gipper" pep talk about how I'm going to be down after the surgery, and I'm going to have time for a couple days, so I'm going to have time to finish this book, and I can do it, and she believes in me…but it was just kind and sweet and in the way I needed to hear it that day.

She might have said, "Listen up, ya fuckin' snowflake. I'm tired of the whinging. Put on your big boy panties. Finish the damn book and be done with it."

Or she might have quoted something Chaucer or Longfellow might have said. I don't remember. But it was precisely what I needed, exactly at that moment.

Being that this was the day before the surgery, I went home and got my laptop, the charger, mouse, mouse pad, and all the gear I needed, piled up on my bed. It was ready for the next day.

When I got home after the surgery, I was jazzed. I was ready to write.

And so I fell asleep.

But when I woke up, I wrote. I wrote and then I wrote more. I went through every chapter and cleaned things up. I polished and polished. I broke my rules about re-reading and re-writing. I fixed things. I went over things I knew the editor would catch.

And I did this to get into the headspace for writing the last three chapters. This was December 29th.

Mid-day December 31st, I was done. Draft number one was complete. I crossed the finish line.

A proud burden was lifted. This is not some great literary work. Let's be honest. I'm lucky spell check and my editor are on my side. I'm an engineer at heart, not a good speller and grammar guy.

But I know how to count a victory, and here it is. I did it. And I couldn't have done it alone.

Contents

Introduction

"So?"

–David Caldwell, my best friend

David Caldwell was my best friend from the moment we met in 9th grade. We didn't know that yet. We just hung around with the same people, we had the same interests, and we peed off the same bridges during the summer.

After a time, people often wondered if we were brothers. David was a lanky 6'4" with the coordination of a stiff drink. I stopped growing at 6'2". When we were together, we were much taller. That's all people noticed. You guys are tall!

"So?" It was David's go-to reply. It was a rhetorical question, mind you. For him, it was a two-letter, single-syllable euphemism for "You've said your piece. Now kindly extract yourself from my immediate presence, continue to the great outdoors, find some exposed electrical wires, and piss on them until someone finds your crispy corpse."

David was lazy about things like this. "So?" was enough. And as we all know, Mary Poppins tells us, "Enough is as good as a feast."

It was not so much that people bothered David, though they did, and it was not so much that he lacked mastery of the English language, though he was an expert. No, it was that David loved to play with his food. A trait we were both cursed with from entirely different genetic pools.

During our high school years, I played football and ran track. (That is to say, I was too familiar with the bench, but I was fast.) While I allowed myself to be punished in practice, David would be practicing his trombone in the marching band.

But we were certain to be in the same Drama courses. Our teacher, the distinguished Linwood Thompson (he is amazing; look him up!), survived our shenanigans over the course of two and a half years.

We snorted chalk dust for one skit. We were punished. We lit up Italian condiment fatties in another skit. We were punished. When trying out for Romeo & Juliet, I read my part wrong and good Mr. Thompson gave me sound guidance.

"Carly! This guy is boasting. He's bragging about his conquests. You're just saying words. Try it again!" And we did.

David read his lines quite well. As I entered braggadocio mode, I also managed to grab my own nethers, much as I thought a boasting fellow of Shakespeare's time would do. David got the part, and I did not. But by this time, our shtick was well developed into our 5-brain system.

As we grew into our young adulthood, David and I travelled different paths for only a couple of years. David went on to serve in his religion of choice, volunteering two years to the cause. In those same two years, I went on to serve my own much-more worldly causes. In this way, we find the only differences between us.

Upon David's return to the not-religious world I lived in, it was like we never missed a beat. The 5 brains were back in action. We completed each other's sentences. We convinced many a mild-mannered citizen that we were sports beat personalities for a major radio station, K-FKNA, located in a city our audience was not familiar with.

Nobody caught on.

No, but they bought our food. They bragged about what a great place Salt Lake City was. They were all in with Jerry Sloan and Stockton-to-Malone. We even convinced one group of Lake Powell partygoers that I was on the practice team for the 1992 Dream Team. How? I had a jersey. A jersey and a quick wit. The 90s were kind to us.

Much of this has nothing to do with the Power of So. It has everything to do with my relationship with David and, hopefully, details enough background such that the reader understands where this came from. It's my story and it's my lessons to teach. And now, the reader should know that we were often up to no good whatsoever. Well... I was up to no good, and David was my chaperone, my protector, and sometimes my mentor. And that leads us to the first time I effectively used the Power of So?

I was an assistant manager for one of the local stores for a nationwide steak and all-you-can-eat salad bar chains. It was good work, and I loved my time in the restaurant business. So did David.

As I managed the night shift, and thus the store's shut down, the crew became close, and we cranked things out. After shutting down the store, we would hang out at any place we could sit down, have some sodas and burgers, or just shoot the proverbial shit. David would show up right at that transition. He was part of the team.

One of those team members, we will call her Alice to protect my innocence, had plans, though. Plans for me. And she would team up with her friends in an effort to capture my attention. It was entirely playful and all in fun. Until it was made clear to me that Alice had PLANS for me. OK, Alice herself told me this, and my unkind rejection was really the catalyst for everything that happened next.

We argued. We bickered. We couldn't agree on the color of the sky. There was friction. Our more senior management team laughed it off and told us to sort it out ourselves. I needed backup, and it wasn't them.

It was David.

As I ranted to him one evening after everybody was gone, he would just chuckle. That didn't help me at all.

"Dude! She's relentless. She's on me like flies on shit!" Too late, I realized I had just misused that metaphor. But David caught it right away.

Laughing his laugh and pointing at me, he finally got the words to come out, "Why do you let her bother you?"

I replied, "Huh?" I was confused.

David then said, "You totally engage with whatever shit she brings up! You need to stop her."

"And how might I do that, O Wise One? I can't just tell her to shut her mouth," I told him.

"No, no, no, Dude," David said, still chuckling. "When she says anything to you, and you don't want to talk, just respond with 'So?'"

Unsure of his meaning, I asked, "So?"

David shook his head and said, "Not the question 'So?' like you want her to explain. 'So?' like you weren't paying attention to anything she was saying at all. Like you don't give a shit. A single word. A single sentence. Watch what happens."

I locked that conversation away and decided I'd give it a try at the first opportune moment. And that moment came the very next day.

I sat with Alice and Bob, a made-up name for our store manager. We were eating dinner after the dinner rush had died away. Within moments, Alice started in with me. That is to say, I probably coughed up something to start her starting with me. I was just as good at taunting people then as I am now[1]. And what is a post-dinner-rush dinner without a little bit of team conflict? Boring. That's what it is.

Alice started, "Do you always have to be rude to me?"

Pretending to be distracted by the absence of anybody sitting behind her, I asked, "Me? Rude? Was I rude?" I said it as if I had forgotten that I had, indeed, just been rude only a few moments prior. It's what I did.

She erupted, "Yeah! I'm getting tired of it." A slight wobble could be detected in her voice. What did I smell? Was that blood? She continued on for a few moments, reminding me how rude I had been.

Playing with the food on my plate and the food sitting across from me, I replied, "So?" And then slowly, I raised my gaze to meet hers, a cherubic, innocent hint of a smile on my face. I held her gaze for a moment...

---

[1] See also Tasslehoff Burrfoot, the kender, and arguably the main character, from Margaret Weis and Tracy Hickman's Dragonlance Chronicles.

In that brief yet somehow eternally slow moment following the locking of our eyes, four thoughts crossed my mind.

First, I wondered if rage-faced Alice was going to erupt into something akin to Vesuvius of old. Second, is there really a vein in the human forehead that should get that big? Third, would this young college student prematurely stroke out of life before having a chance to enjoy her 20th birthday?

Finally, I thought to myself, "So this is the Power of So!" Somehow, I casually raised a deep-fried shrimp to my mouth, having first dipped it using expert aim, without looking in the crimson, tangy cocktail sauce without breaking the silent war going on between our eyes. The crunch of the panko breading seemed inordinately loud, like so much thunder.

As Alice sought any appropriate response, the moment lasted just a bit too long. Our store manager started laughing. He declared, "You two are like brother and sister!" Then he stood up and walked away, probably also wondering about the proximity risks with Mount Alice looking closer to an epic explosion.

The Power of So? Yes, indeed.

In that one-word sentence, I told Alice that I was disinclined to bear any concern for whatever verbal harm I had inflicted nor for any rebuttal she could contrive. Indeed, nothing she had to say had any value whatsoever until I allowed it to. Not only did I tell her that in one word, but she also received the message loud and clear.

I share that story here because it was the cause of many future laughs between me and David. Not only was it funny to us, but it embodied the Power of So? And I was no longer a Padawan of So? And somehow, Alice and I remained friendly combatants in that same brother-sister way until I left that restaurant. I haven't seen her since, and I hope she is doing well.

The real meaning behind the Power of So? is not to willingly dredge up and revisit such a grand tale that I only wish I could see Alice one more time to remind her of it. No, it's to describe the liberation that follows. It is critical to many of the anecdotes and lessons here. Sometimes I call them rules, to fully embrace the Power of So?

It is my filter. It is how I clear away the mud and the noise so that I can see the real problem. It's how I stop Alice from making sounds so I can enjoy my fried shrimp. It's how I can interview a distraught customer and filter out all the blah blah blah to get a firm understanding of what must be solved.

So many of these lessons are predicated on the ability to eliminate the noise, see through the mud, and pinpoint where your focus should be. *The Power of So* clears the way, just as a great leader will empower their team by clearing roadblocks in the way of progress.

There was a time when I was managing a support team. One of my distant counterparts was a manager for one of our consulting teams for the same product we supported. She came to me with a problem her consultants needed help with.

They had gone through solution after solution. All were valid. All took months to complete. We had to negotiate to get higher asynchronous limits for a tool they would use and would need to continue to use for up to nine months.

As we went back and forth, I asked about constraints. They couldn't use it this way or that way, and the UI was too limited to be helpful, and so on. I kept using my Power of So with each perceived hurdle and roadblock. So? You can't do it this way. So? You can't do it that way. So? So? So? And as the clutter left my mind, I had a thought.

"If you can create the script using this asynchronous tool, and it will take the tool almost nine months to run, could you also list all of the filters, projections, etc., to be converted to an SQL statement?"

She replied, frustrated, "Yeah, we could do that. We have it so fine-tuned that it would be easy to create a SQL statement."

A light came on.

I told her, "If you can create a SQL statement that you are 100% certain will provide the same outcome as updating the data across nine months using the UI, we can take details like that to the DBA team and see if they can run it overnight."

The Power of So. And it got me kudos from our consulting team and our DBA team. The customer was pleased that we saved them nine months of consulting fees.

It is my filter. Or it is my way of filtering.

For you, the reader, it is imperative to find your way of filtering. If it's the Power of So, then so be it. Whatever it is, it must be consistent, reliable, and to be honest, unoffensive. Note that it is far different from apathy.

Apathy is a lack of interest. Apathy is not caring. The Power of So is to be so selectively caring as to ignore anything that is not germane to the problem before you. And that is a carefully worded definition. Accept what is and toss it aside. Don't ask for more about what doesn't matter. With *The Power of So*, we weed out related matters, similar concepts, and bring focus to what is relevant to the problem.

Indeed, the Power of So could be defined as acute, intense, ultra-focused caring, with no respect to any peripheral details, but with a crushing curiosity to uncover and further filter or include as many details as are needed to solve a problem.

The following chapters contain more anecdotes, sad, cynical humor, true stories, and perhaps one grotesquely embellished tale from my life. For the greater part, I've changed names where I hope to avoid paying anyone for the artistic liberties I have taken herein. I often use Alice and Bob, though absolutely none of the people I name here were named Alice and/or Bob. Or maybe they were.

The important thing to remember is that as you read, you will sense patterns. Patterns I didn't even realize existed in these lessons or in the real world. And then it takes one person to say, "This is happening over and over and over again! It's like a huge pattern!" You may or may not subsequently realize they are exactly right.

Ask the right questions. Show me. What are we trying to solve? Blueberry the shit out of that thing. Seek to understand. Ask the right questions. Show me. What are we trying to solve? And so on. You'll see the patterns. You'll find the value.

And hopefully, you will receive some great compliments from an important person that other important people believe you solve problems faster and see things clearer than anyone else they've encountered.

This, my friends, is the basis of effective, efficient problem solving: filter out the noise. This is the Power of So.

Do a Good Job:

Important vs. Urgent

"Do the best you can until you know better. Then when you know better, do better."

– Maya Angelou

"It's a trap!"

– Admiral Akbar, arguably the worst war strategist aligned with the Rebellion

This chapter is one that is difficult to swallow. In the next 3000 words or so, I will relay to the reader a single sentence my great mentor said to me. I will eliminate a cornerstone function of businesses around the world. As Morpheus did for Neo in The Matrix, I will help you free your mind.

On top of that, I will solve anthropomorphic climate change, solve all political problems on the table today, and I will give you the winning lottery numbers.

The second paragraph is a lie. I can't do most of that. So, let's get right to business.

Yes, business. There are numerous immutable facts we can

agree upon, generally speaking. For example, I can say humans require food, water, and breathable air to survive. All things being equal, that is true. There may be variations on that statement that make it untrue, but we probably can agree it is more than a reasonable statement. It is an immutable fact, all things being equal.

Other immutable facts seem to include the following examples. Like, cats freak out when you surprise them with a stealthily placed cucumber. Fact.

If I have dinner with my sister on her patio, some random bird will shit on her. Then she will tell the false tale of someone stealing her dessert one long-ago night in our childhood when we stayed at our Nonna and Nonno's home. Without getting into the details, none of us brothers ate her dessert. Nonna believed my sister. The bird thing happened once. Okay, this is not an immutable fact. It just happened the other night, and I wanted to share it with you. That poor bird. My sister's poor blouse. Neither is okay. When she reads this, I will get no more homemade calzones. Ever. That part may become an immutable fact.

But more immutable facts include things like a certain global fast food chain's ice cream machines always being broken. Science deniers will always reject scientific findings like climate change. Corporations never will care about you, the employee, as much as they say they do. And organization charts are everywhere.

The last one in that list, org charts, is what I wish to disrupt.

Or at least the way you view them. If you want to do a good job, blow up your org charts.

Years ago, my most amazing mentor, whose name I do not share here, said in passing something to the effect of org charts being largely useless. I remember looking at him, probably with no small amount of "What the...?!" written in neon letters across my face.

Org charts? Largely useless?

Yeah. He was right. They are, for the greater part, useless. You would do well to take note.

Org charts are the ubiquitous basis for "who's who in the zoo." They tell people "the structure" of the business. Org charts describe head counts, and they align with job functions. We see, ultimately, to whom I report all the way up to the top. Or sometimes, who are my direct reports, and their direct reports, and so on, until you hit the ridiculous bottom of an outdated concept of hierarchy. Add in something about matrixed teams, and it suddenly becomes Management by Bowl of Spaghetti[2].

And that is all an Org chart is. Hierarchy that gets in the way of progress, value, and growth, smothered in deceptively delicious tomato sauce and Parmesan cheese.

As I dwell on this lesson, I find only one or two real uses for

---

[2] I will trademark that soon.

an org chart. The first is to tie work roles, positions, entitlements, etc., for proper Enterprise Resource Planning (ERP) setup.

The second use for an org chart is to give the wrong people the wrong idea about what's wrong with their current employer. Really smart people get caught in that trap. You know them. We all know them. They gripe about not having enough people working on X. And X can be development, support, sales, janitorial, or whatever really triggers you.

Really, org charts should make you angry. The kind of angry you get when you're halfway through your meal, and you find someone else's eyelash in your food. And you're eating alone in your home because your ex ran over the cat when they made an unannounced, uninvited visit to your home while you were at the office.

Stupid, the-straw-that-broke-the-camel's-back angry. Org charts. Angry.

Are we there yet? No? We're still in Chicago/Peter Cetera territory. They released a wonderful song in 1984 on the Chicago 17 album. The key lyrics from Hard Habit to Break are:

Being without you

Is all a big mistake

And that's what you're saying to yourself right now. "I've always had an org chart, even when I was fixing those damnable ice cream machines at..." Old habits. The voices, they tell you to go back! It's a mistake! No. Do not listen! It's all okay.

Or you think trashing org charts is right up there with the time you thought it was a good idea to go skinny dipping in the icy cold waters of a remote pond at Camp Crystal Lake with your new romantic interest. And your concern isn't that troublesome, Voorhees kid or your bad decision-making paradigm.

Well, you're wrong. Get out of your comfort zone. Blow up your org chart and start thinking differently.

For every team I manage, this is the given guidance:

You do not work for me. You work for you. You work with me, not for me. I do not work for my manager, regardless of if they agree. I work with them. That turns out to be true all the way to the name of the company that appears with your automatic payroll deposit.

Within the teams and departments I have run, this mentality makes an incredible, empowering synergy. Those direct reports in the org chart just became empowered to do their job. They feel confident in discussing improvement opportunities with peers and the team in general. The manager suddenly is more like a quarterback or coach leading the team instead of a team owner smoking cigars while sitting in an office directly linked to a global shortage of mahogany. Each ex-direct report can now own something, fix something, or challenge something. The dynamic is breathtaking when it kicks in.

We see it all the time in sports. And when my bones worked well for me, I played a great deal of basketball. I never understood the commitment it takes, the time, the drive, to go all Magic Johnson, clearing snow off the driveway and practicing for hours in the cold. No, that wasn't me in my youth, but I get it now. I learned it during my time at the gym, pickup games, city league games, and such.

Talk with your team. Nobody needs to be atop a hierarchy. We just need to actively describe the game plan, our roles, and our team process. Then we let it work. As we refine that process, which really is talking during the action, then capturing lessons learned, our outcomes translate to wins.

It was not unusual at our team's best to hear someone encourage the low post player to cover the baseline. Adjust. Not from management in a hierarchy but from a team member. Someone else defending a fast-break yells, "I've got balls!" and the other person knows to cover deep or on the wing. Or maybe a shot goes up, and the defender barely scrapes their finger across the ball just enough to change trajectory. "Block!" Now, people on the team know to adjust immediately and adapt to the new outcomes.

None of that requires hierarchy or words like direct reports or org charts. Nobody stops and looks at their fellow defender and says, "But you're taller and your role is Center, and you should really be near the basket and not out guarding the ball. My job is to defend the foul line out to the three-point line." No. That team would lose. Always. Because of concepts rooted in an org chart.

As we filter out the noise that comes from an org chart, in my experience, knowledge authorities are elevated and leveraged properly in our team's tactical operations. Tenured team members begin to see opportunities to contribute more to team success. The org chart manager becomes the quarterback or point guard, picks your sport, and ensures we all know the game plan, our roles, our rules, and our constraints.

Then, everybody participates in the execution. No more "in the trench" people. Everything is team. Team this, team that. How can we improve the team? Where can I help the team do better? And we shrug off those old org chart roles.

Perhaps right now, you are thinking something like, "But, Kev, that's only a little difficult. I could make that change."

Sure. You could. It's not hard.

Now, tell your team members they are empowered. Need time off? You're empowered. Mental health day? Empowered. Time out of the queue for compliance training? You're empowered. Indeed, set up your business rules to automagically approve such requests. Discuss it as a team. Describe the constraints.

One example I mentioned was compliance training. While we will get to Important vs Urgent at a later time, it is critical to know the key difference between the two. It is critical to ensure your teams know the difference. Here we go: Core job description stuff, urgent. Compliance training, important. Do the important stuff first.

How can I easily tell which is urgent and which is important? Simple.

Let's say Alice and Bob work in a warehouse. Two trailers just showed up. The first contains produce. The second contains ice cream. The produce must be moved off the unloading dock within 30 minutes of unloading due to heat and a risk of vermin. The ice cream must be moved to the freezer within 10 minutes of coming off the trailer. It is clear to see what must be done first. Moving the ice cream to the freezer is urgent! It will melt within mere minutes. Sure, there is risk with the produce, but process and policy indicate we have more time to let the produce sit.

Now in that same scenario, the forklift driver accidentally drops a case of bleach, which spills across the floor. In the ensuing chaos, the driver forgot to lock down the forklift. As he urgently helps to control the hazardous spill, his forklift rolls into a couple of cases of ammonia, and the containers break open.

The ice cream starts to melt. Chloramine gas will be created the moment the bleach and ammonia start to mix.

Which problem is urgent, and which problem is important? This is not so simple, dear reader. Let's press the pause button and ask Mr. Webster for some help.

Urgent, adjective

Definition of urgent

ur-gent|\'ar-jant

1a: calling for immediate attention: PRESSING, urgent appeals, an urgent need 1b: conveying a sense of urgency

2: urging insistently

Important, adjective

Definition of important

im-por-tant | \ im-por-t-nt, especially Southern US and New England -tant, -dant \

1: marked by or indicative of significant worth or consequence: valuable in content or relationship

2: giving evidence of a feeling of self-importance

Ice cream and chloramine gas. Which is urgent, which is important?

If Star Wars' Admiral Ackbar were sitting with you, his vast, fishy mouth duct taped for reasons known only to yourself, he would be bouncing in his chair, trying to tell you something. But you don't want to remove the duct tape. And we all know that given the chance, Ackbar goes on and on.

Anyway, allow me to help.

Both the ice cream and the chloramine gas are urgent situations. Looking at Webster's definition, both are "calling for immediate attention." That didn't help at all.

But there is a difference.

Looking again at Webster's definition, though this time we read the definition of importance we read "marked by or indicative of significant worth or consequence... valuable in content or relationship." Let's pick a few keywords from that definition. How about worth, consequence, valuable?

Hopefully, you, the reader, caught yourself before you said, "But Kev... ice cream and human life are both valuable!" While that is undoubtedly true, I will not be the person equating the value of ice cream with the value of human life. You do you. I'm going with humans every time.

It is clear that the saving of human life in an unfolding hazmat scenario is urgent. One might even argue there are time constraints, which create greater urgency. I do not disagree. Indeed, if we look again at the definition of urgent, it speaks of immediate attention. Think deeper, especially if you have worked in a contact center. There, we always speak of urgency. "Treat this ticket with urgency!" What do we mean?

Time.

Urgency, its implied immediacy, is all about time.

Importance is driven by value. I contend that the latter half of the definition even suggests values with an s. Now, given the view that we are not talking ice cream vs. chloramine gas, but rather 10 minutes to melting vs. saving human life, it should be clear to see that urgency always takes a back seat to importance. Don't forget the poor veggies came in third place. That doesn't mean they were neither to be treated with urgency nor were they unimportant. They simply came in third place.

Why did we go through that? Remember now that you were telling your newly liberated team made up of people who are mentally self-employed, "Core job description stuff, urgent. Compliance training is important. Do the important stuff first."

In every single contact center I've helped fix, this is an immutable fact. Unliberated direct reports do not feel they have time to complete training. Even that compliance training HR is yelling about. No time. They talk about being too busy. This is a dead giveaway. "Too busy." Anyone who claims to be too busy is working strictly by time-driven urgency and not value-driven importance[3]. As a leader, step in and fix this with urg... well, it's important to fix this right away.

In any event, it is all too easy to get caught in the trap. Is it coincidence or irony that has the definitions of two critical words so similar as to feed the trap? Yet, understanding the difference between value and a deadline makes all the difference.

Here is a practical example with a bit more real-life application.

Assume Alice is working service requests. Because Alice is amazing, her personal backlog is at zero. A mere 10 minutes before her shift ends, she refreshes her backlog view and sees two Severity 1 service requests that were created at exactly the same time. These service requests have a contractual agreement requiring her response and guidance within 15 minutes.

Because we know that urgency is really a matter of actions driven by time, we know that these service requests are urgent.

---

[3] Look up "mere urgency effect". Find out how you should have listened to that damned Admiral Akbar just that one time. Then prepare to change the way to log victories more and more every day. And then forgive me for using a wee laughable example of chloramine gas and melting ice cream to make a point. I love ice cream. I hate chloramine gas. Long story, and not for this book. Also look up the Eisenhower Matrix as an easy quadrant-view of how to better classify your tasks, workloads, deadlines, by using Important/Urgent, Important/Not Urgent, Not Important/Urgent, and Not Important/Not Urgent. It makes a massive difference as you transition out of the mere urgency effect trap. Otherwise, not my area. Read someone else's book for that. I just found something that has helped me solve problems better through the years. Whatevs.

Just then, Alice's Tibetan mastiff, Bob, noses his way through Alice's 13th-story window that overlooks the canal separating her high-rise luxury apartment building from Arkham Asylum. Should Bob leap mightily from the window, there would be no saving him from the fall or freaky chemicals in the canal. Alice has only a split second to determine which is urgent and which is important!

I know I promised an example with a bit more real-life application. I can't help myself sometimes. I know that nobody in their right mind would name their Tibetan mastiff Bob. But that doesn't detract from the situation. Filter out the noise! (More on that later. It's almost like...patterns....and links....) Do we save Bob or review and respond to both Severity 1 service requests within 15 minutes?!

Of course, we save Bob. We love Bob. Bob has value in our lives more than service requests. And though we get paid to work service requests, no reasonable manager would ever suggest we work service requests over letting Bob fall to an unknown doom in the canals surrounding Arkham Asylum.

So that's a lot of clowning around to get to a point. Your team. Not your direct reports but your team. They are empowered. They can drop out of the live queue to work on training, compliance, or whatever we, the team, have determined is most important. When there is a question, ask the quarterback. Ask the point guard. If it makes you feel better, ask the coach. Ask any team member. If you have done this right, you're all on the same team. You will always get the same answer.

Now, either out of a lack of patience or a fair grasp of my ramblings, we are at a point where we operate as an empowered team. We know the difference between important and urgent; we get done those things that bring or reward value and values, and that adds to one incredible outcome: a whole bunch of people doing a great job. Something they believe in. Something they can get behind.

Everybody understands the importance of their work and makes choices to serve the team and the company with whom they work.

This is a much better option than feeling like work is indentured servitude. Believe me. You've been there too. This is how we commit to doing a good job.

Get Paid:

Love what you do because you work for you!

"If you're good at something, never do it for free."

–Joker, The Dark Knight

Strangely enough, to me, this is a difficult chapter to write. Almost everybody has heard the phrase, "Never do business with family and friends." Well, that phrase or something very close to it. I think it's a bunch of baloney, regardless of how many tragic anecdotes one can find. Humans grew into the world working the family business until families could support the children or other endeavors drew the children away. Argue this all you want. It's not entirely germane to the chapter. It is only here as a start, and so I can draw a line, almost like saying something is out of scope in the world of project management.

You likely also heard another one that goes something like, "Love what you do, and you'll never work a day in your life."

One of my favorites is, and I'm quoting myself here, "Every day is Monday or one day closer to Monday." If you want to suck the life and happiness out of a group of people, make that statement during Hump Day celebration or TGIF Day when everybody wears jeans and a shirt covered in a hibiscus print. Yes, remind them of the stark realities of this cruel world. You will quickly become the arbiter of fun and not-fun in your workplace. And people will leave your burritos untouched in the office fridge.

No, the point of this chapter is, well, us. You and I. Individuals. Not the folks working the family farm. This chapter is about people who may or may not have left home, who have entered the business world, and for some accursed reason have to work with someone else or sell something to someone else. Us.

Once you narrow it all down, there are key things to remember about your job. These are true whether you are well into your career, just starting out, or retiring into a life of regrets, what-ifs, climate change, and a broken Social Security system.

I'm reminded of one of my all-time favorite movies that stars John Cusack. Let me be clear that you could put John Cusack in a movie about microwaving a bucket of guano before pouring it on your hash browns and ice cream sandwich, and I would still not only watch that movie, but I would enjoy it, too, because... John Cusack. But that is not the movie I am talking about. If Cusack went so avant-garde, I am sadly unaware. Instead, I am talking about the iconic 1989 underdogs-can-win movie titled Say Anything.

Among the many quotables from this masterpiece, one sticks out relative to this chapter. In an amazingly written and performed scene, Cusack's Lloyd Dobler is awkwardly sitting at the dinner table with his post-high school love interest, Diane Court. Also present are Diane's father, James, played expertly by John Mahoney, and a couple of James' friends.

It is clear from the conversation that Lloyd is there to be with Diane. Also clear, James and his friends are from a different economic pool than Lloyd. Maybe call it upper-middle class. Lloyd lives in an apartment with his sister and her son.

During the dinner conversation, the spotlight inevitably falls upon Lloyd. Not because James or his friends really wanted to hear what Lloyd had to say, but rather because Lloyd makes an observation about the relationship between James and Diane. He admires it and shares that he has nothing like that in his life. The moment creates more awkwardness, and Lloyd steps away from the table.

In the next room, Lloyd notices and compliments James' jukebox, then asks how one might obtain such a gadget. After some not-so-humble banter, James' friend asks Lloyd what his post-high school plans are.

Like a vulture that has been watching its prey futilely crawl away, James pounces with a slightly derisive, clearly condescending, "Yeah, Lloyd. What are your plans for the future?"

Lloyd responds epically (go see this for yourself) and does a short verbal dance with James. Easily one of the best earnest Lloyd Dobler moments of the entire film. But when he realizes that James is not asking about the future, but rather capital T-The capital F-Future, Lloyd provides such an incredible Lloydism. It happens like this:

"I don't want to sell anything, buy anything, or process anything as a career. I don't want to sell anything bought or processed, or buy anything sold or processed, or process anything sold, bought, or processed, or repair anything sold, bought, or processed. You know, as a career, I don't want to do that."

The moment is incredible as he finishes describing what he wants. And since he can't figure it all right then and there, he really just wants to hang out with Diane. The beautiful answer that it is, it's clearly not the answer James wanted. Lloyd basically just told James that every day is Monday, etc, and James realizes how true that is.

But this isn't about James. If James had his way, there would be no story here. No wonderful movie. No songs about Joe. And no wisdom from Lloyd's friend, Corey. She gives the hard-love line to Lloyd, "The world is full of guys. Be a man."

By Odin's silvery, thick, curly leg hairs, I love this movie.

Now we're back to the title of this chapter, the quote, and the story thus far. It feels like there are a couple of key principles munged into one. And yes, you are right if you feel that way. If you don't feel that way, nobody can argue with your feelings. Remember that. You're wrong, of course, but nobody can argue with your feelings.

There are a couple of principles here that make a huge difference in your career and in your life. They're important.

First, let's take the title and quote and make them into one sentence.

Love what you do because you work for you! If you're good at something, never do it for free.

Since you already read the chapter on doing a good job, let's take that part out. You're already committed to doing a good job. That leaves us with this:

Love what you do because you work for you! ...Never do it for free.

The three parts of this lesson are these:

1. Love what you do.

2. Never do it for free.

3. You work for you.

Let me be honest about something. My career is something I Forrest Gumped my way into. I exited the exciting restaurant business, which is really the only job I had post-high school and bumbled my way through the scenic route to working in WordPerfect's 1000-seat contact center. Free support for everybody! Jesus himself was throwing out copies of WordPerfect to everybody, like so many fish and loaves of bread. Everybody had a copy, and nobody paid for support. Those were exciting days!

I got that job because for three reasons: a friend worked there, I had self-taught myself through to a Certified Netware Engineer (CNE) certification, and I had no clue what I wanted to do for a living. Then babies started rolling in, as they tend to do in Utah. Time was passing, and for my part, modesty aside, I was exceptional at what I did.

Out of training, I was placed on the WP Networks team, where I supported our products on any freakish abomination of networking conceived to date. That included something called Moses Lan. But also Windows NT, Novell Network, and more. It was a big deal to go from training to that highly technical team, and there was only one team more technical and more enviable to be on: OS/2 Support.

And so I earned my way there. Then I was moved to the team that just supported all WordPerfect products except their email platform. Still, I excelled. Then, I was hand-picked as one of 12 support representatives who would pilot the first pay-for-support WordPerfect service. It was $25 per issue, regardless of the product or environment. My success continued, and I was again handpicked to be a new support team that would operate outside the norm as we aided the existing Novell GroupWise support team in recovering from disaster.

I Gumped my way into this, and five years later, I felt like a master of my realm. Oh, most people from that environment will tell you I was an a-hole, and they would be right. I learned here the difference between confidence and arrogance. Putting that aside, I loved what I did. It was the start of my career and before that job interview, I never would have thought this was the direction my life would go.

Detour back to high school. I had an *ok* ACT score. Good enough to go almost anywhere I wanted. My curriculum included courses on health professions, and I was in pre-calculus as a junior. I ably warmed the varsity football bench and ran track. I was a two-year president of the Men's Association, and I thoroughly decry the membership requirements today. Chess Club. Drama Club. Some Who's Who book of US high school math students.

I wanted to be a Navy doctor.

I wanted to attend Annapolis. I wanted to be an officer. I had been told all my life by teachers and counselors that my intelligence was off the charts and I could be anything I wanted. It fed my ego, these words. In my junior year, instead of filling out scholarship applications and even trying to get applications out to my preferred universities, I asked the local U.S. Navy recruiters to lend me a hand.

Oops.

They did a wonderful job building me up. Take this test, Kev. 99th percentile. Take another test, Kev! 99th percentile. Then the Army recruiters called. "We heard you were talking to so-and-so... Come take some tests..."

By the time I stopped taking tests, the Army was asking me to sign up for DLAB (I had an insane aptitude for languages), and there was an appeal to the Army's pitch. Again, 99th percentile. The Navy stepped up their game and helped me with two things that would be one of the single most impactful decision-making moment of my life to that point.

I introduced doubt to my first passion and suggested perhaps Naval ROTC would be a better option. "Sure, Kev. We'll help you with that," the recruiters said.

And then, about a month later, they called and excitedly told me that there was some kind of nuclear test I needed to take that, if I passed it, I'd be a shoo-in for the ROTC.

"But beware," they warned. "This nuke test is calculus and physics. It might be a bit more than you can handle."

Those guys knew hubris. They knew me. I took the test. I got this!

I passed. My sin is not intelligence. My gift is intelligence. My sin is hubris.

Another month later, my letter from the NROTC board arrived. "Dear Mr. Carly... we believe you are a better fit for our nuclear program, and as such, we regret..."

In anger and confusion, I joined the Army as an 11BC2. I didn't finish boot camp due to a gigantic hemorrhoid from hell.

Let me be clear: I admire the humans who serve. I don't admire what I did. I did it for the wrong reasons, and I went in the wrong direction. On the upside, it eventually dropped me in the lap of WordPerfect because some Navy recruiters teased my ego, and I rebelled against life. And I failed.

I went somewhere I didn't love. I signed up to do something I didn't want to do. I did it for the wrong reasons. It was a true formula for failure.

As we fast forward back to now, I can look back on a more-than-30-year career that has been far more successful than any measure any executive might seek. I was fortunate because I accidentally stumbled into doing something I actually loved. I found it at the intersection of technology, customers, and solving problems every day, over and over again. It never got dull! I was doing something I loved. I was good at it, but never was I satisfied.

Something was always missing. So, I pushed my way out into the world and grew. I finished my undergrad, and I got into management.

Oops... -ish.

I wanted that management title. I wanted the power, the responsibility, the control to make change, make things better, and lead people along the way. And I was really good at this stuff. Some of the greatest career moments, accomplishments, and kudos came during this time. I loved the attention. I loved what I was doing. And something was still missing.

Along the way, I became quite the wage earner. At times, I had been billed out at a rate of $280/hour due to my expert knowledge in certain specific matters. I worked for some of the largest companies in their respective vertical markets. I had the names of industry leaders on my resume.

I finally got it.

I loved what I was doing. I was getting well paid. It didn't matter. At least, it didn't matter until the last piece of the puzzle fell into place.

Yes, I worked for industry leaders. I took their money in piles. My resume looked outstanding. Except I was always working for someone else.

What? Like, was I a W2 employee?

No. Not like that. It's more of a mentality change.

Had I realized this earlier, during my WordPerfect/Novell time frame, I would have told you that I don't work for WordPerfect or Novell. I work with them. And when I became manager, I should have explained to every "direct report" that org charts are for silly rabbits. Our team works together. Our team has a leader, but each of us has a shared accountability for executing the game plan.

This is a constant 1:1 meeting and professional development material. We work together. We work with other people at Company X. Indeed, we work with Company X. When you get it, it liberates you.

Remember, the days of a gold watch at your 40-year retirement party are things of the past. They are gone. People change jobs like they change underwear. That started in the late 1990s when the dot.com bubble burst. Suddenly, subject matter experts were putting in a few months at one company, then a year at another, a few months somewhere else. And it wasn't always by choice. This is when layoffs as a normal course of business came about.

My experience started with a company where my director wrote in my annual appraisal, "Kev walks on water. His can-do attitude is backed up by what he accomplishes within our team and with our customers."

At that same company, only a few months later, our CIO wrote an email to our HR Director, asking, "Who the fuck is Kevin Carly, and why the fuck does he make so much money in Utah?!"

She was asking some good questions right there. She didn't care what the answer was. Her decision was made.

This happened a few more times, exclusively due to economics and not my performance, mind you, over the next 15 years. I learned from Corporate America that I can be the most excellent of team members. I could be the guy who saves the day every time you need to get me involved. And like that, I'm gone like Keyser Soze. Here's some severance so you don't futilely sue us.

And let me tell you something, Corporate America: I learn freaking fast.

And I'm grateful that Corporate America can't actually read. So, it's pretty easy to say that in a threatening way, and nobody will care.

This was my transition to being a hired gun to fix up contact centers, not like contract work, but by reputation. I could filter out all the noise, and I could filter through all the data, and I could fix your contact center. This is what I was made to do in so many ways. And so that is exactly what I did every time the layoffs came around.

I'd take my severance, drop right into a new job, fix things up within a year, take my severance, drop right into a new job etc, etc. I'd sit with a company for a few years, then rinse and repeat. I learned to work for me, and regardless of the curve balls Corporate America threw my way, or if those balls came from the economy or wherever I was prepared. I volunteered. When the open-pit mine at Kennecott caved in back in 2013, I volunteered to leave. That saved a job for one of my peers. He knew it, and he kindly thanked me for it.

Nice guy, sometimes. But it is all selfish. When your employer no longer has leverage over you, when they are no longer your master or overlord, they have nothing. You are in control of you. You make decisions for you. You work for the best human you could possibly work for. You.

It is liberating, as I said.

Sure, they will pay you. But when they ask if you will do extra, you can ask, "What's in it for me?" and their answer can't be just money. Why? Because it is no longer about the overlord's part of the employment contract (aka money). You are neither slave nor chattel. It's about you. You work with your employer, not for them. And if they want you to do more of something that's not part of your 40-hour work week (and it's 40 hours because I get my job done, and done well, in 40 hours), then you can go all Darth Vader on them, like when he's telling Lando Calrissian where the bear shits in the woods.

"I'm altering the deal. Pray I don't alter it any further."

You work for you. If your employer doesn't like it, get a new employer. Why? Because that's exactly what they will do to you, and they will do it for egregious reasons. Like, "We didn't make enough billions in profits this quarter, so we will lay off 5% of our staff, including this a-hole right here." Or, at a shareholder's call, someone points out that the dividend was $0.03 short of expectations. Of course, your employer will lay off some percentage of their staff... including this a-hole right here.

It doesn't matter how great you are or how high quality your work is. It doesn't even matter if you serve a critical function within the team. Corporate America will toss you out like so many dirty diapers just to keep investors and shareholders happy.

Maybe this is a call for unionization everywhere. If someone picks up that flag, I'm right with you. That's not my point.

No matter what, conduct your life as if you work for you. Prepare financially to be out of work for a few months. Always, always, always, interview. Even if you don't intend to change, keep your interview skills sharp. Keep your ear to the ground. If there is something that makes you unhappy, walk away. Do it for you.

It's Never Personal:

Keep your friends and survive your job.

"It's not personal, Sonny. It's strictly business."

–Michael Corleone, The Godfather

That's one hell of a movie to borrow a quote from and use as a lede for a chapter. As things turned out for Sonny, it got personal. Well, for the entire Corleone family, it got personal. When you mix family and business, it gets personal.

That's not what I'm talking about here, though I am Italian.

No, I am talking about filtering out what happens in your standard run-of-the-mill workplace. There may be a few sub-lessons herein.

Many of my lessons and rules were refined in contact centers and the world of IT. It is fair to say that there was some amount of hostility involved. Let's be honest. Customers, that includes me and you, can be some righteous assholes. I, and the teams I've managed, have served some real award winners. Though I clearly have no problem with all manners of usage of the English language, some of these I will spare the reader the fullness of the customer's language.

- "I know how to find where you f***ing live."

- "I'm gonna kill your dogs, your wife, your kids..."

- "F*** you, you f***ing b****! You don't know s*** about this system[4]!"

"Let me talk to your f***ing manager. After I'm done, you won't have a f***ing job in this industry!"

That's just a few examples. These comments really happened to humans who really worked for me. They did. Believe me, I go heels for my team. The outcomes of these particular threats were not what the callers expected. And though my team members may, in that moment, feel protected, the trauma of such interactions may not immediately leave them. Indeed, they may linger. Could a customer find their home? Are such threats real? Are their families and pets in danger?

---

[4] This real-life ornery customer comment earned a heroic retort from the support human who self-reported her response and asked if she was going to be fired. She used language taboo even to my tongue in defending herself against verbal abuse and misogyny. As I teach my own kids, once the rules are broken, all bets are off and anything goes. I'm unsure which traveled farther, the upward distance of my eyebrows or the downward drop of my jaw. Regardless, I returned both to their normal position and congratulated this woman for standing up for herself, then asked her to return to work. I did advise that it's best to get a manager involved next time rather than verbally retaliating.

The probabilities are incredibly low. Aside from maybe Gru, most of your typical bad guys don't announce their actions before committing them. Freeze ray! No. They are documented making the threat, reported to management, and now reported to their management. Probably nothing is going to happen at all.

But the words, the threat, linger. We need to filter them out. Don't let it get personal.

Now I'm no psychiatrist. I don't even play one on social media, nor do I feel like one after spending the evening in any particular chain of motels or hotels, no matter how much I like their marketing campaign.

I'm still waiting for someone in the U.S. House of Representatives to ask aloud, "Is there an actual, legitimate, concerned-about-the-United-States lawmaker in this chamber?" And perhaps 90 percent of the House yells out, "No, but I did stay at a Holiday Inn Express last night!" Somehow, that just wouldn't surprise me.

I digress.

My point is: I'm no psychiatrist. I cannot tell people how to filter out the pain. But I do tell my teams to filter out often. Keep telling yourself Rule #3: It's never personal. It's never personal. Never let it get personal. Never.

This is something you must discipline yourself to believe. That's not me being a psychiatrist. That's me telling everybody that's how I did it for myself.

I've done this from the time when my angry, alcoholic, ex-U.S. Marine, Italian father would yell at us when we were kids, though I knew he was angry at himself. Or when I waited tables and a customer's steak was not cooked correctly. They weren't upset at me, but I was the person who got yelled at. Or when a customer would call the technical support line when their documents were corrupt. Not my fault at all, but it was so easy to vent their frustration on me, the guy who answered their call.

Go through the exercise many times, and understand the principle of the *Power of So*. And how they intersect at never letting it be personal, and it seems a natural lesson, indeed.

You say you want to barbecue my cat. Sure, sir. Probably gamey but go ahead. I recommend Purina Dry Kitty Rub. How may I help you today? Your job is on the line, and you're going to eat my liver? OK, Mr. Lecter, Shall I reserve a table for two? Meanwhile, might I ask you to press Function F2... that's right and now CTRL+F10... yes... is that working? Uh huh. And can we try to print? Which wine did you want with my liver? With my cirrhosis, I recommend avoiding a young varietal like Beaujolais. Oh, it's printing? And you're skipping my liver tonight? A wise choice for both of us. Shall I cancel the table for two? Yes sir. Don't you mention it. We all get frustrated now and then. Yes sir. You make it a great day now. You're very welcome. Buh bye.

Disaster averted. No hard feelings. Play along as if it's normal, then take control. As in take control away by playing the same game. It makes the scenario ludicrous. Maybe by taking control away, you can even have fun. This works for me.

Regardless, interpret this how you will. Find your own path. Your own way. Whatever mechanism works for you is the way that you prevent people from controlling or influencing you. Own your reaction to their stimulus. That reaction is yours to control. And you can let it go in one ear and out the other. You don't need to process it at all.

I tell my team members to avoid any human language and interactions with Human Resources. Filter out all the noise however you will, by whatever means you can, and focus on the substance.

When you set aside all the noise, all that is left is the facts. And when all you have is the facts, you have all you need to solve the problem.

So many of the lessons and rules herein are interrelated or intersect. Some of them seem to be a retelling of other lessons. In some ways, they are. As I wrote in the introduction, it's more like patterns.

And patterns are retellings of themselves, aren't they? Sometimes they are smaller, sometimes larger, but a pattern is a pattern is a pattern.

Similarly, a filter is a filter, be it preventing something from being personal, seeking to understand a challenge that lay before you, asking the right questions, or even keeping coffee grounds out of your favorite mouth. All you are doing is filtering out the noise. A pattern. Focus.

Once your filter works, there are no personal feelings hurt.

Perhaps it's a bit more difficult when it's team members rather than customers. Those conflicts may be more difficult to filter out when they are face-to-face or when the relationship carries more weight and substance. Indeed, at the time of the writing of this chapter, I'm two weeks past being hung up on by one of my closest and most valued peers.

Yes, it still happens. That guy knows a proper jerk when he hears one, and I've got game. Plus, fortune favors the bold. His rude disconnect from our Zoom session actually caused us to solve the problem he didn't want his team members to own. Sometimes irony can be so ironic.

Nevertheless, we must continue to filter out those moments. Why? People have crap days. Stress, deadlines, bad traffic, or whatever. Who knows? We're in a virtual world these days, and it's more and more difficult to tell what our peers are going through day in and day out. We're disconnected.

Moments like these are simply noise to be filtered out. Turn on your filter. Don't let these things be personal.

Ask the Right Question:

Filter Out The Noise

"It is more important to ask the right question than to get the right answer."

–Peter Drucker, Austrian-American educator

"As you learn to consistently filter out the noise and ask the right questions, you create the fastest path to finding the right answers. Asking the right questions empowers you to solve problems more efficiently."

–Kev, that one guy who wrote this book

Most of the chapters in this book are really just euphemistic anecdotes and exposition for filtering out the noise. This chapter is that. More so.

For this chapter, I will share a story of a friend presenting to me a riddle in a game of 20 Questions. I asked one question and ruined his day. Do not underestimate the power of one single question.

The riddle was presented to me by a most distinguished and knowledgeable human for whom I have a great deal of love and respect, both professionally and personally. This gentleman never reported directly to me, though I found his insight and assistance always valuable. He maintains a keen intellect. As time passed, we became close friends.

As best as I may recall, this is how the interaction went.

One day, my friend entered my office and was eager to share something with me. He explained that he had heard a brain teaser of sorts and wanted to run it by me. As it was, technical support people should always be interested in such things. That's what we do, in a sense. Someone tosses us a problem. We ask questions. We solve the problem.

Games like 20 Questions resonate with us because we like to solve problems by narrowing down the possibilities. If I cut a room in half horizontally, to be sure, this will narrow down the number of things that could be the answer. Do it again, but vertically this time, and in two questions, the player has quartered the room and dramatically cut down the number of possible answers.

For this brain teaser, I was presented with this scenario: You are walking through the woods when you happen upon a cabin. As you peer into one of the windows, you see a number of dead people inside.

And then the problem to solve: How did they die?

Now, if you have heard this before, that's fine. You already may know the answer. That's not the point. The point is I had never heard the riddle, and I didn't know the answer. Consider it in that light.

For those who haven't played this game, you're missing out. You are presented with a question, a scenario, or a problem to solve. You get 20 questions of the yes/no variety. By the time you reach 20 questions, you must solve the problem with the information you have acquired through your good questioning. Finishing a smaller number of questions is better and gives you bragging rights to your deductive reasoning skills.

Back to the brain teaser.

As I often do, I codified or categorized the elements of the scenario. They must be broken out and defined in an effort to determine their relevance. Are they noise? Do they matter? Filter out the garbage and focus on what remains.

This is how I play the game. I broke it down.

First, I was walking through the woods. Both walking and woods could be critical elements. If I were rock climbing or sky diving and happened upon a cabin with dead people inside, that could have some incredibly strange implications. Still, walking and woods. I collected them in my mind and moved forward.

Next, I happened upon a cabin. Happening upon a cabin in the woods is not an incredible or unusual event. In fact, it's quite normal in most situations, I thought. Yet, codify, I must. Happening upon something is materially meaningless. It has no value whatsoever. The cabin, not so much. Therefore, what happened was round-filed, and the cabin was added to the mental collection.

Moving through the puzzle, the next part had me peering through the windows of the cabin. No matter how I thought through this, I could think of nothing material about peering through windows. That's what we do just before we flee from the police. It is otherwise inconsequential, and so I filtered out that piece of the puzzle and then moved to the last part.

We finish with seeing a number of dead people inside. Being that the question following the puzzle is to determine how the people died, a number of dead people just isn't germane to the puzzle, but neither is it on the periphery. We simply see dead people. Not in that M. Night Shyamalan way of seeing dead people. No, this is just a number of dead people. More than one, and probably more than two.

The "dead people" element is explicit in the asking of the question and will be explicit in the answer. I must keep that. However, "a number" is strange and ambiguous. Is it relevant? Maybe. Filter mode is on, *dead people* is a keeper, and "a number" is gone for now.

So, what am I left with?

Walking through the woods, I looked through the window of a cabin and saw dead people inside.

Now, it's time to define these words. There is nothing odd about walking and woods. Nor is there a problem with woods and cabins, as well as cabins with windows. Surely, there is a problem with dead people in any cabin, but we will just slide that aside for now.

We're left with walking, woods, and cabin. In my head, I wondered, "Is there a way any of these words don't fit with the others?

The quick answer that came to my head is that walking is reasonably clear, as is woods. Cabin, however, could be ambiguous. Now, I am neither a dictionary nor a thesaurus, to be sure. But I have some wonderful memories of staying in a cabin in the woods. I also have been in the cabin of a truck. I have stories not for the faint of heart about a cruise my second wife and I took and the cabin within the boat upon which we were cruising. We're on the Carnival Wall of Shame somewhere in the Pacific Ocean, I'm quite sure.

All the same, the cabin became the focus. The ambiguity of that word demanded clarification. I needed to narrow it down, but since I had only a limited number of questions, I needed to be most effective with my inquiries. I wanted to do more than ask in a way that cuts the room in half, then half again, and move on ploddingly. Thus came my first question:

"In terms of purpose and function, does this cabin belong anywhere in the woods?"

The smile on my friend's face suggested I had sucked all the joy and sunshine from his day. He looked a bit injured. A disappointed sound exited his mouth, "No."

Well, now I had something. This cabin didn't belong in the woods. That allowed me to trim down the possibilities. No log cabins here. Arguably, a truck might find its way into the woods for hunting or camping purposes, but the cabin's purpose and function do not allow it to be found anywhere in the woods. So, it's probably not a truck. What is left?

A boat. Boats have absolutely no business in the woods. But how would a boat get to the woods? Would a boat generally have windows through which I could peer and see a number of dead bodies? I pondered having a boat at Camp Crystal Lake, which is surrounded by the woods. Such a boat would not likely be fitted with many windows at all, if any. As I added windows to the boat, the boat grew and became even less and less likely to be there where I was walking through the woods.

That left me pausing with my next question. How much more information do I need, or have I extrapolated enough that I'm confident answering the riddle, having asked only one question?

I thought of another friend, one from my childhood and teenage years. He always said, "There never was a 3 a Carly was afraid to shoot!" He was right. In the game of basketball, I loved the big shot. And so I saw the 3-point shot in front of me, and I took it. I offered to solve the riddle.

The number of dead bodies are inside the cabin because their airplane crashed in the woods.

And that slammed the door on my friend's hope for a good day. With only one clarifying question, I solved his riddle. There was no more fun for him to have. That is until I said let's see how my team does. Sunshine re-entered his life.

One by one, we called in another team member and asked the same riddle. Typically, these paid professional troubleshooters got to about six questions and threw their hands in the air. The questions were all over the place. Nobody aside from myself solved that riddle. That was a different problem for me to solve.

It is important to note that not everybody is a natural-born troubleshooter. Not everybody is cut from the cloth that is made to solve problems in this manner. Some of it can be trained, to be sure, ipso facto in this book.

In my time as a contact center and IT operations leader, I've hired steakhouse servers, biologists, archeologists, public school teachers, and more to work in roles they had little familiarity with, and we worked together to help them be highly successful in their new careers. These are people with portable skills I find to be critical to their professional development and success on my teams. None of those backgrounds are overtly problem-solving roles. All of them solve problems in the course of actually doing their core jobs. Or rather, they filter out the noise and garbage so that they can continue in success with their jobs.

Given a proper mindset and attitude, these people can be taught the concept of asking the right question, which is easier than trying to teach how to troubleshoot agnostic of a platform or problem. Maybe it's me, but most people I discuss this with tend to agree. You can't really teach troubleshooting, but you can teach people to ask a question or three. Or six. Or even as many as 20.

However, these same people tend to argue that the concept is applicable only in the context of your own knowledge. That is absolutely close to the truth. Really close.

I could not walk into NASA and solve the challenge of time or space travel in 20 questions. Not my area. And that's not what this chapter or even the Power of So is explicitly about.

Explicitly, no. Implicitly, yes. Engineers, or people with that engineering mindset, will understand the difference here. People with different flavors of intelligence, while perhaps not being born problem-solving extraordinaires, may still be quite skilled with framing a problem and solving it.

As my father once told me, when I was young enough to believe he made it up, he said, "Necessity is the mother of invention."

Invention is a euphemism for providing a solution to a perceived problem.

Entrepreneurs are great at ideas, and sometimes those ideas involve inventions. Sometimes, those ideas are sourced from other people. But ideas don't solve problems. Ideas are what give entrepreneurs a chance to add wealth to their lives.

But it is the engineer who makes the proverbial rubber hit the proverbial road. Don't confuse the two. I made this clarification with purpose.

The world has a need for entrepreneurs. They translate ideas into business, then into revenue, and then into wealth.

The purpose of an engineer is far more than this and in much greater need.

As we drill down on the ideas presented by entrepreneurs, it is the engineer who brings us prototypes, feasibility, and such. When the world wants to solve problems, they don't look to entrepreneurs. They look to engineers.

I recall a business trip I took to Denver, Colorado, around the autumn of 2013. As I awaited my flight, I saw a familiar face and approached with my hand out. A recognizable human in the mining and energy business, Kelly Sanders was awaiting the same flight back to Salt Lake City. He recognized me from my time with Rio Tinto and KUCC. It was a great opportunity to catch up briefly with a very good person and a strong leader.

We got to the topic of my family, and I led with an update on my eldest son and his enlistment in the Utah Army National Guard. We spoke about his future and how he had not yet pointed himself in any direction. Kelly offered sage advice. He told me, "If you have any influence on your children, help them move into any kind of engineering role that appeals to them. That is the future."

It seemed generic enough then, but I understand him now, not through any kind of epiphany, but through observing the world day by day and occasionally turning off my *Power of So* filter.

This world is being abused and used up, and not one single nation on this space rock is doing enough to stop the pillaging of our planet. Not yet.

And when the time comes that people get saddeningly and soberingly serious about protecting our home, it will not be entrepreneurs they look to. It won't be shiny, slick sales professionals. It may not necessarily be directly the masterful CEOs of the world, though they will surely be involved.

No, it will be the engineers, ultimately, who fix our situation. You may call them scientists, astrophysicists, civil engineers, or whatever. But one thing will be certain. They will solve problems, and they will get there by filtering out the politics, the media, the civic divisions, and the imaginary national boundaries that keep separated the diverse human family.

And those engineers will get there faster by asking the right questions and filtering out the noise.

Show Me: Use your team!

"Great things in business are never done by one person. They're done by a team of people."

–Steve Jobs

"Trust but verify."

–Loads of people

Stop! Collaborate and listen!

–Vanilla Ice

Some of the most successful moments in my career have been when I used three particular team members, friends, really, to bounce ideas off of. One is the same as David mentioned in the introduction. The others are Steven and Dean, whose last names I will not mention here. Stevis and Deanis, you know who you are!

When we collaborated, magic happened. I contend we filled each other's gaps of thought. We bolstered each other's thinking. The ideas we conceived became more solid with each other's reviews. Truly, it was powerful working with these humans. To this day, I miss working with these people.

I encourage everyone to find their best collaborators. Find someone honest on your same level or better to backstop your ideas. Someone who won't let your rare moment of crap slip through the cracks. Watch your productivity and quality skyrocket!

As a leader, build your teams this same way. Remember, as you build your teams, do so with the mentality that you are working with these people. They are your experts. Your equals or better in capability. And the way you leverage these team members is to bounce ideas off of them and encourage them to do the same. Soon, you'll find yourselves in a constant scrum of productivity and problem-solving, where the sum is greater than the parts!

Hopefully, that's a motivating intro for this chapter. It's an important part of the book. Many leaders have said the quote, "Trust but verify." It's sometimes hard to be on the receiving end because it can be heard as if it actually means there is a lack of trust. The opposite of what's being said. Though that's not the intent, I prefer something else: Show me.

Nothing in that two-word, simple sentence indicates a lack of trust. It merely says, "I want to see it." Two words. No misunderstanding in that at all.

And in this book about filtering and solving problems, where we are focusing on solving problems more effectively, the concept of "show me" is powerful. "Show me" is how I eliminate confusion. It is how I learn more about your progress. "Show me" is how you get me on the same page with you. "Show me" is a status update for your project task. "Show me" is clarification.

"Show me" is a filter.

One particular project I was working on had the task of building a system that responded to client requests. The response fed the client with a text string of coordinates that were sourced from another system where the data was collected and formatted from various sources and stored in a secure database to keep it over-simplified.

I had decided to virtualize the environment, and this was at a time when virtualization was fairly new.

While I had documented this well enough for the systems people, and they knew what to do, I had not done the same for the executive team. They didn't have a clue what I was doing, and that was entirely my fault. They knew I was doing words words words environment virtual something words more words, technical mumbo jumbo sounds expensive what's the budget more words, etc.

In that, I had failed. In my update, where I provided words on paper, I was called to book for a lack of information. I quickly looked at all the words I provided and was amazed that words didn't provide information. As fast as I could, I switched to listening mode as another technical guru started saying he didn't think virtualization was such a great idea.

I interrupted and asked some questions, starting with, "Which part of this is causing you the greatest concern? There is a lot of information here, but clearly, I've not provided what you need to hear." And, of course, they had keyed in on this virtual environment stuff.

I grabbed a dry-erase marker and drew a poor representation of what the system would look like. My explanation started with apologies for my lack of artistry and moved swiftly to the low cost of virtualization. I mapped out how we could use the SQL server here, the web server there, where the firewall would sit, and so on. It took perhaps five minutes, and all concerns were addressed.

Embarrassing for me. I could have used a slide show to assuage their concerns before they existed. One simple picture mapping out the concept of the system my engineers were building out would have done the job.

At that moment, the "show me" rule was created. Just show me.

Understand that "show me" is not "make me read it" or "read it to me." No, "show me" is more like "walk me through this thing!"

If you can generate an error message, show me how you get there.

You can cause a failure? Make it happen right now while I watch.

You cannot load that data? Let me see what happens.

Let's go through the log file together.

Even actions like, "I've created this script and I am confident it covers 100% of the requirements. I want to show you how it works" is an example of "show me."

The concept is such that you are not alone. Use your team. This has nothing to do with trust. It has everything to do with using another person's filter to validate your own filter's output. OK, if you want to call that trust, fine. It is collaboration. I call it quality. I call it improving your filter's performance.

That's why it's a chapter in this book!

The Where and When Rule:

Thank you, Covid-19.

"Ubiquitous really bad comments from out of touch executives and analysts regarding return-to-the-office quote here. Why? Because they said workers performed poorly during the pandemic and are going to get fat if they keep working from home."

–Lots of CEOs

Bullshit.

–Me.

I don't really need to remind anyone of the rampant fear and resulting shutdown and work-from-home following the COVID-19 pandemic. No, I'm not that guy that will say things like, "I told you so." However, I am the guy who will tell you that I am, indeed, not that guy who will not tell you things like, "I told you so." There is a difference, subtle though it may be.

Long before that nasty virus came to be, I had a rule that kept me focused on results. Not time, not a clock, not a location. Just results.

I could have kept it really simple and called the rule "Focus on Results," but where's the fun in that? I wanted to make a point.

Too many leaders are often focused on the wrong thing. One contemporary issue, though I'm loathe to include it here (and when has that really ever stopped me?), is the State of Colorado Supreme Court's decision to keep former President Donald J. Trump off the 2024 presidential ballot due to participation in the 2020 insurrection.

This was a decision based upon language in the U.S. Constitution's 14th Amendment. Look it up yourself, but it is quite plain. Take the oath, be involved, you are no longer allowed in the playground. It's a result of the Civil War. And ex-President Trump did just that, no matter how you spin it. I'm not a Supreme Court judge. They may decide differently. Politics, and whatnot.

Not long after Colorado's top court made that decision public, the former Governor of New Jersey, Chris Christie, made a statement. He said, "I don't think a court should exclude somebody from running for president without there being a trial and evidence that's accepted by a jury that they did participate in insurrection."

This is a prime example of leadership wrongfully focused on the problem. The problem is not the Colorado Supreme Court decision. No, they did determine he was involved in the insurrection and was subject to the definition of the 14th Amendment. So? They are not excluding Trump from running for president.

The fact is that by being involved in the insurrection, Trump himself, by his own actions, excluded himself from running for president. The Colorado Supreme Court merely confirmed that. Christie has it all wrong. He needed to clear his filter and focus on the real problem.

That problem? A court decision? The unknown decision of a pending yet another court trial? What voters may or may not want? The price of rice in China? No, no, no, and no!

The problem is Trump's actions when compared to the ultimate law of the land. When held to the candle of the Constitution's clear verbiage, Trump's actions fail the test. His own actions make him ineligible for office. That's not my choice as an unaffiliated voter. It's the clear fact when I, as an unaffiliated voter, read the Constitution, I understand why the 14th Amendment was put in place and when it was put in place.

Again, I'm not a judge and this is not my area… Moving on…

How does this apply to the workplace? My rules have existed long before Trump was POTUS. As long as I have been in a leadership position, I've preached that one should not focus on when and where. And then COVID-19 came along.

And then we were sent home for a couple of years.

And then we were gaslighted by so many business leaders and analysts. It's true. Now, to save my own hide from litigation, I'm not naming anybody here. You can look up the comments and observations. There was a period of high performance, unprecedented performance, even. People working from home did very well, and one might say even morale went up.

Work-life balance skyrocketed, according to anecdotes from my own vast circle. People were able to deal with family matters, school, and put in more work hours without the inconvenience of a commute.

And then suddenly, around 2022, execs and analysts were calling for a return to the office and there were executive articles popping up declaring how unproductive workers were. One article even famously described how unhealthy working from home would be in the long term.

I looked again at my own team. A powerhouse of performance. I checked in with industry peers. High morale, high performance, healthy turnover. Sure, there were layoffs in the marketplace. There were economic factors out of our mid-management control, but within our fishbowl range things were actually quite good!

But my own teams, they ride the crazy bus. I have had the latitude to drive my own deliverables. We have managed to meet expectations, over which I have had a great deal of short-term control. And where that control existed, it has had nothing to do with time. It has had nothing to do with when or where.

I have kept the team focused on what really matters. Results.

What are those results? In each position, it's a matter of context, to be sure. Mainly, however, it is customer satisfaction. Really that is king. Do what must be done to keep our customers happy, whomever they may be. Does that have anything to do with where or when? No.

We do not focus on geography. We do not focus on the clock. We focus on getting the job done in a way that pleases the customer.

What does this mean?

In my role, I have had engineers around the world working in my organization or department. I work very hard to eschew stringent details like organization charts, punitive, draconian scheduling rules, and policies restricting where and when a team member works.

Some readers might be crying bullshit right now. Stay tuned. This is real, and COVID-19 proved my theories right. It reminds me of a pre-COVID interview I had. Just 10 minutes in, one executive let out a burst of air and exclaimed, "This is all theory! What will it cost me to find out if you can prove it works?!"

"Well," I calmly replied. "It's not theory. I've already proven it works, and it works well. You can wait for the book and pay whatever I decide it costs, but then you'll only get stories of how it worked, which isn't exactly what you're asking for. Or you can hire me, but now there's a doubt-modifier I'm going to add to the base salary that indemnifies me against your inability to get out of the box. If you really want to find out, you have to pay, and your impatience is a red flag for me." Needless to say, his impatience was more powerful than his desire to blueberry, and my tolerance for the bullshit that comes with impatience is non-existent. That was a poor match, and we couldn't come to a compromise. He's waiting for this book, and their business shut down somehow while suckling upon the government teat.

In any event, my teams deliver results outside of the old-school rules of geography and time. They do not operate in an office from 8 to 5. As a result of the pandemic, they currently work where they want. I have an expectation of "coverage".

We have a game plan that has terms like *demand* or when the customer exists and asks for our help, when other parts of our global team meet demand and do not meet demand, which time zones our team lives in, which meetings exist and what expectations we have to meet.

There are other factors, but as a team, we work together to assign coverage. None of this depends upon who is in which office or any location specifically. We do not care which beach is being used. Indeed, our definition of location has words like security, privacy, and such. Those words define the location. Not words like latitude and longitude.

As such, the team is empowered to be wherever and whenever they want, so long as expectations are met. Be that demand, meetings, assignments, security, etc. And, of course, we keep our customers happy.

How is that? We are not focused on where and when. We are focused on results, and COVID-19 validated our ability to work this way.

The Craig Brown Ladder Lesson: Temet nosce.

"Know yourself. Don't accept your dog's admiration as conclusive evidence that you are wonderful!"

–Ann Landers

Don't worry. I don't speak Latin. I merely find temet nosce to be a fascinating concept. There is well-documented use of this concept's value that can be traced back to the ancient Greeks. In another form, it was inscribed at the entrance to Apollo's temple of the Oracle at Delphi and is one of the Delphic maxims. It is attributed in varying forms to ancient sages and philosophers. Socrates and his student Plato made use of it in their teachings. It even makes an appearance in the movie The Matrix as it hangs over the doorway to the Oracle's kitchen, in a clear parallelism to the Temple of the Oracle at Delphi. For this chapter, it is more important to know one of the many meanings behind temet nosce and why it is so critical to personal and professional growth. The context presented here is specifically recognizing your talents, competency levels, skills, weaknesses, and such.

Early in my career, I ran into this lesson in a very personally humbling way. I was young and in my 20s. Having a rudderless couple of years, I landed a job with incredible benefits. I had access to tons of technical training as well as tuition reimbursement.

This was a smorgasbord of growth opportunities, and I was starving.

Technical certifications started falling into place one after the other. I worked graveyard shifts because it allowed for a lot of approved study time if there was no work to be done. I was cruising!

But suddenly, one of the benefits of the job was rejected. I discussed this with my manager, who tried to be quite calm about the discussion. When he explained why my request was rejected, I escalated to our company's Human Resources department.

Don't judge me. Looking back, I was that employee. Not that going to HR is bad. It was how I went to HR. And I was standing firm on my point. Mainly, my reasoning was financially driven, and I felt that the facts showed I was owed a lot of money that my manager refused to approve payment. My unfiltered youth, steaming Italian blood, and my bank account met at the intersection of Don Vito Corleone and his daughter's birthday. I was the rainmaker! I was going to beat the big company that disrespected me!

The kind, competent, and professional HR Manager I met with treated me with respect. He listened. He asked questions. He sought to understand. When we were done, he coordinated a meeting between my caustic self and my department director. The HR Manager attended to facilitate.

The meeting quickly turned a bit hostile, and the HR Manager found himself mediating for nearly 45 minutes or an eternity. I can't clearly remember. It was a long time. The HR Manager was outstanding and patient. A real pro.

The meeting wrapped with the old me insulting the department director's knowledge. That was enough to stop any hope for compromise or concession. Again, ashamedly, I was that employee. Thankfully, the interaction that was to come the following week really became gold for me.

The HR Manager set up a meeting time in his office. Just the two of us would be there. I was nervous. I knew I had crossed several lines behind my hubris. When I entered the HR Manager's office, I was shaking inside, uncertain of what punishment would follow.

Instead, the HR Manager calmly and methodically walked me through the events, through my financial request and the reasoning behind it, and then through that terrible meeting with my department director. He asked me if that sounded right, and I eagerly agreed. He really took outstanding, detailed notes.

Then he changed course.

The conversation moved to me and my performance in the team. In an earlier meeting, we had discussed this, but it seemed he wanted to cover it in detail once again.

Let me tell you how amazing I thought I was. I was incredible. I listed all the great things I had done for the team. I talked about my assignments and how the scope of my work was inherently volumes more than that of my peers. As I verbally dumped all of this onto the HR Manager's desk, burning up the HR Manager's time, the HR Manager merely listened, took notes, and politely asked for more detail when he felt it was appropriate.

When I finally took a breath that indicated the completion of my narration, the HR Manager put his pencil down, leaned forward, and coupled his hands together. The posture indicated that I had something coming and I most certainly earned whatever it was.

The HR Manager proceeded to explain to me his experience with corporate employees. He went into detail, some of which I cannot recall any more. I do remember being transfixed and somewhat confused.

I expected some kind of punishment or penalty for my behavior. Instead, the HR Manager was explaining something so important that it stuck with me and evolved into this lesson.

Almost verbatim, the HR Manager spoke back to me about my tenured highlights and majestic performance. Listening to another person speak my words left me feeling aghast. It was horrible to hear.

I shrunk as I listened.

The HR Manager then explained how he participates in so many employee reviews, discussions about performance, and merit increases. One of the most common problems he hears are rooted in the appraisee's view.

He told me how almost every team member argues about how wonderful they are, how well they perform, how much they contribute, and how the team will fall apart without their radiant greatness. He continued on with how so many team members crumble under a more accurate review of their contributions and skills. It is so hard to hear you are not great. Even when that message is delivered with kindness and a gentility usually reserved for explaining bad behavior to fluffy newborn kittens.

This was not a condescending tongue lashing. The HR Manager was truly, earnestly trying to help me understand that I was a good team member. Good, not great. And in fact, there were some things I really needed to improve upon if I wanted to be viewed as really good at my job. He brought forth commentary from my direct supervisor and the manager with whom this conflict started. There were as many positive comments as there were opportunities for improvement, or even outright negative-but-honest criticisms.

As he wrapped up that part of the conversation, the HR Manager told me how important self-awareness is and that knowing which rung my feet were on with the corporate ladder. If I didn't firmly possess that understanding, I would run in to similar problems again and again.

While the primary purpose of the meeting was dealt with to my satisfaction, I was summarily humiliated. Maybe it is better to say humbled. To be certain, I needed this lesson. I needed to hear it. Inwardly, I vowed that I would seek to know myself in a way that would solidify my standing, regardless of the rung upon which I stood. And with that knowledge, I would know for myself what was needed to grow. Or rather where my roots were when I needed to transplant them.

I have found throughout my career that most of my managers cannot disagree with my self-evaluations. I do not find that to be an observation of hubris or arrogance. I merely know how I am doing in my work, my work quality, the value I add, and more. Indeed, this self-awareness is a humble position for finding the most opportune pathways to personal and professional growth.

The next chapter picks up at this point for greater clarity.

Now, if you are paying attention, I referred to the HR Manager as HR Manager. I didn't assign a name like Alice or Bob. I didn't change his name to protect his innocence. In fact, I won't do that at all. Why? I hope you are wondering.

The reason is that as we wrapped up this tremendously valuable session, we shook hands. I looked the HR Manager in the eye. I said in a genuine, earnest tone, "Thank you..."

And I blinked. I froze. After the phone calls, the in-person meetings, the conflict, and the resolution, I couldn't remember his name. It was right there on the door I had walked through several times. I failed to recall his name mid-sentence in a moment of gratitude for what this human had done for me on several levels.

He maintained the handshake and laughed as he said, "It's ok. My name is Craig."

We laughed and parted ways, never again encountering one another.

After some time of chewing on this lesson and sharing it with others, I decided not to call this the temet nosce lesson. It felt perhaps a bit elitist, what with being words from a dead language and a concept debated among philosophers from time immemorial.

The thing that always stuck with me was what the HR Manager's name truly was. I don't remember his name. I didn't then and I don't now. When he told me his name in that embarrassing moment, it may or may not have been Craig. For some reason, that is the name that stuck with me when I reflected on the personal impact of this lesson. And so, the HR Manager, Craig, was also awarded a last name: Brown.

It might have been Smith, Johnson, James, Arthur, or anything else. I really don't know, and I'm ashamed of that to this day. He deserved better from me.

Thus, I will forever carry the guilt of that moment of accidental disrespect. I'll have no way to seek him out and find a way to apologize or thank him for how that interaction affected me so profoundly. He may never know the legacy he created in that moment. Craig Brown, whatever his name is, deserves to have a lesson named after him.

Craig Brown taught me that I should know myself. Know where I am on that ladder everybody is climbing every day. Failure to recognize where I am means that I cannot establish a starting point for improvement. Those attempts would be nothing more than screaming into the face of a hurricane. Futile. Wasted time and effort.

Temet nosce. Know thyself. And thank you, Craig Brown.

The Gardening Lesson:

From temet nosce to Tomato Roots

"A tree has roots in the soil yet reaches to the sky. It tells us that in order to aspire we need to be grounded and that no matter how high we go it is from our roots that we draw sustenance."

–Wangari Maathai, Environmental Activist, and first African woman to win the Nobel Peace Prize.

At the writing of this chapter, I am pleased to announce, "Spring is HERE!" I love spring. Spring is rain, rebirth, and a transition into some of the best temperatures of the year. My grass is green. My garden is ready for planting.

Ok, I'm an optimist. Spring is coming. It's like Monday. Every season is spring or one season closer to spring.

Wangari Maathai's quote is profoundly true and such a wonderful match for this chapter. The imagery in this quote is that a tree reaches the sky, but no matter how high, it's really about the roots.

The placement of this chapter is not a mistake, either. In the Craig Brown chapter, we took a journey through one of the not-so-proud moments of my life. I thought I was a top-shelf employee. I was the only team member who worked solo, which felt to me as a large bit of trust tossed my way. Yes, hubris is my sin.

And as the chapter wrapped up, there was a lesson to be learned: temet nosce. Know thyself. But is it enough to merely know yourself?

Self-awareness is a great thing, and its importance to me is clear as I wrote an entire chapter about it. I contend, however, that it is merely a piece of a greater puzzle. And that is how, when riding my crazy bus, we get to gardening.

I am Italian. That is to say, I identify as an Italian. My father and his parents were Italian. My mother was half Italian through her father. Of my eight great-grandparents, six were Italian. Having taken the DNA test from a leading genealogy company, my genetics indicate that I'm left with between 50 and 60 percent Italian DNA. And I am a third-generation US citizen.

So, I'm not actually Italian, but I identify as one.

All the same, the mythology around Italians is generally true, as far as I can tell. I adopted into my lexicon the use of mythology to describe rumors (true or otherwise), truths (depending on your perspective), and realities about the subject. In this case, one mythological element about Italians is that we cook. I prefer to say we were born with a tomato in one hand and a bottle of olive oil in the other. And with the exception of one Italian I know, maybe he's a relation, and maybe he isn't, who doesn't cook.

Now, when I say cook, I don't mean mac and cheese. I don't mean sauces made out of a can and with no other ingredients. And I certainly don't mean expert knowledge of heating things in a microwave. No, I mean cooking with ingredients, the use of a stovetop or equivalent, a crazy collection of herbs and spices, no real commitment to written recipes, a truckload of patience, and an indifference to tasting off the utensil you might be stirring with.

Italians cook. Most of us, anyway. We love food. We love eating it almost as much as we love preparing food for the Feast of San Gennaro or even just for 40 people or so. Italians who are reading this are just nodding their head and mentally listing all the other things I could have listed in the last paragraph. Yet we probably all have the same basis of a recipe for Sunday gravy gnocchi, and by Odin's studded leather eyepatch[5], we know what a pizza really looks like. And on a tangent, there is no better pizza on this planet than a pizza Margherita[6]. To me, it represents the simple

---

[5] Ok, this is one of those mixed metaphors I like to irritate people with. Sue me. "By Jupiter's blazing electric thunderbolt" just doesn't have the same panache. Besides, that same DNA test showed I'm like 3% Norwegian, too, so I can swear by those gods as well, right? Right?

[6] Yes, for those who are familiar with Italy, Italian cuisine, and maps, there are

approach to Italian cuisine, but the taste is simply incomparable.

In his youth, my Nonno (or grandfather to you mortals) was moved back to Italy after his turn-of-the-century birth. He grew up in northern Italy, where you can still find families with the surnames Carli, Magnino, Aimonetto, and more. During his time there, he grew up on a potato farm. That news always smelled off to me, but it might have explained his dislike of most things potato-y.

My Nonna (do I need to explain?) was the real gardener, though. The back fence of their property was always flush with these delightful-looking purple grapes. The garden always had so many vegetables growing. In the yard were flowers, cherry trees, and the place where we played bocce with Nonno. Certainly, some of my fondest childhood memories are in the yard and in the garden my Nonna kept. Nonno's pidgin English was sometimes difficult to follow, but Nonna was always crystal clear. And make no mistake about it. When Nonna spoke, you listened. She was like the old E.F. Hutton of our Italian family. Some may remember the old television

---

two Neapolitan references in this chapter despite the fact that I said my nonno grew up in northern Italy. Historically, there is a bit of a difference, northern Italians to southern. Naples, or Napoli, is the source of all things Neapolitan and is in the southern half of Italy. It is the resting place of San Gennaro and the origin of pizza Margherita. I value this linkage as I am also descended of the southern Italians on my maternal grandfather's side of the family. Plus, there is the whole Queen Margherita of Savoy, the Italian unification, and the pizza Margherita colors of red (tomatoes), white (mozzarella cheese), and green (fresh basil) mirroring the flag of Italy.

commercials from the 1970s where the actors were in a hectic, busy environment with noise coming from every direction. The actors were talking about what their investment advisors told them. Invariably, the last actor said, "Well, my advisor is E.F. Hutton. And E.F. Hutton says..."

And the room always fell deathly quiet as every person in the camera's frame turned to look at our last actor. When E.F. Hutton speaks, people listen.

And my Nonna, too.

So, when Nonna is talking about her garden, we listen. We were children, yes, and we had a small insect zoo just outside her back door, but we listened with a sober seriousness. I loved Nonna's garden. The smell of a tomato plant instantly takes me back. Tomatoes are, thus, my most favorite thing to grow in my garden.

Nonna graduated from the School of Hard Knocks. I never saw her diploma, but that wonderful woman knew so much about life and gardening. Nonna taught me many things about gardens and growing things. That's just about where this lesson can start and, really, I will somehow tie this all back to the Craig Brown chapter. Really.

One thing Nonna taught was that if you are transplanting tomatoes, you must bury the plant deeper than how it was last lifted from the soil. In fact, if you are transplanting, bury the roots low enough to cover at least the lowest level of leaves. Depending on the size of your plant, it could be a couple of inches. Some gardeners, Nonna said, will bury even more than that! Sideways, even!

So, the roots had to go into an even deeper hole, at an angle, and burying the leaves.

Now fast forward almost three decades later. I was passing on Nonna-knowledge to one of my children. We were at this same point, when my son asked what would happen if we just buried the roots so the green parts of the plant would benefit from photosynthesis. He was smart. If memory serves, he was in 4th or 5th grade, and he wasn't so sure that Nonna's School of Hard Knocks taught about things like chloroplast and photosynthesis.

For the briefest moment, I wondered if his elitist, left-wing, modern education would have caused precocious insult and affront to my Nonna's knowledge or if she would have laughed it off and wondered how such vermin ever descended from her. As the thought passed, I asked my son what he thought would happen. He explained that more green leaves getting sunlight would help the plant grow stronger. I handed him one of the transplant tomatoes and told him to plant it 12" away from the last one I planted. I told him to plant it the way he saw fit so that it would get the most bang for its sunlight buck. And so he did.

The roots were perhaps 1-2" deep, and by the gods of sunlight and color palettes, there was as much green showing as could be. He was meticulous. Precise.

The next day, his plant had fallen over, roots tipped away from the soil. Probably some wind had blown through, or perhaps it was an animal creeping through our garden. Regardless, where he put his roots did not allow for growth.

I proceeded to explain to him that placement of the roots is everything to the plant, and with so many plants to choose from, each might have its own needs for placement. It is critical that we know where the roots are to be placed if we hope for maximum growth or at least reach as close as possible to the plant's potential for growth. In a garden, that means food.

And I realized at that point that my Nonna taught me an incredible and poignant lesson. When I piece the Craig Brown lesson to Nonna's tomatoes, the realization is profound.

The gist of the Craig Brown lesson, if you will remember, is to know thyself. Know who you are, where you are, why you are there, and so forth.

Once you know where you are, you can grow. But to grow, you really need to be certain that your roots are well placed, the right depth, the right distance, and even if the plant must be staked or caged to aid with support for lush and plentiful fruit.

Similarly, in life, it is not enough to simply know where you are or why. Failure to place your roots properly will not facilitate meeting your maximum potential. Shallow roots may cause you to be knocked over, or your growth will be impeded.

That knowledge passed from my Nonna to me and to my son. Now that I have grandchildren, I will pass it on to them, as well. While one might scoff at the wisdom behind tomato roots and how critical it translates to life or that knowledge of tomato roots is part of the chosen legacy of any reasonable leader, I can only tell you, the reader, that this lesson is arguably the most important of this entire book. And when the leader properly prepares the environment for growth, the environment filters out the noise that otherwise impedes or slows down that growth. Growth becomes natural and part of the culture.

Know where your roots are in life and in the workplace. Make sure you have them positioned properly. Treat them well and let them grow deep. As Maathai said, "...in order to aspire, we need to be grounded and that no matter how high we go, it is from our roots that we draw sustenance."

Kevin Carly

The Jimmy John's Lesson: Service Always Trumps Resolution

"So, does the destination matter? Or is it the path we take? I declare that no accomplishment has substance nearly as great as the road used to achieve it. We are not creatures of destinations. It is the journey that shapes us."

–Brandon Sanderson, Author

This lesson is a frequent visitor in my conversations. Leading contact centers at any level, even as a front-line team member, is to be flooded with variations of the word "resolution", though this is also about life, solving problems, and empathy.

First contact resolution, or FCR, is a foundational measurement with a high correlation with high customer satisfaction. Indeed, it is widely considered to be, arguably, the pinnacle of measurement that influences customer satisfaction upward.

The data doesn't lie. FCR is important. Why? Because "resolution" is implicit in the creation of a service request, ticket, work order, or whatever you may call it. I make a service request because I want to resolve a problem or a question.

But I contend, as a bit of a disruptor, that FCR, while critically weighted for higher customer satisfaction, is secondary to the customer experience. The customer experience is far more difficult to define and measure. But when you embrace this concept, doors will open before you.

This chapter is longer because it is so important. I'm not saying the other lessons are not important or even less important than this. No, this chapter is longer because it takes a few stories and scenarios to plant the right seed.

Consider taking a much-needed vacation to your favorite destination. When you return home, you have friends and family over to see pictures or videos of your trip.

And all the pictures you have are of your return home.

Surely, you are saying, "Wait a tick, Kev. Nobody would do that. You take pictures of you and your partner in the water with dolphins. You get a close-up of the giant banana spider and its sprawling web you saved your spider-fearing wife from walking into. Maybe you have a few ironic shots showing you eating lasagna at an Irish pub in the Bahamas. You might even have a few frames of tourists being rescued from the angry Pacific tides of Cabo San Lucas that came from behind to interrupt their perfect beach snapshot." Right? Well, I've got those pictures. Maybe you don't. But we're talking about what FCR is about, not the good times on my vacations.

FCR is about creating a help request and having it resolved while needing only one single contact between the customer and the service engineer or representative, or even when automation can resolve a customer's query in a strict Question-Answer or Issue-Known Resolution scenario. That is FCR. FCR is not about the journey. In my vacation example, FCR would have included the start of the trip and the end of the trip in a manner that is satisfactory to the customer. Or you. Now, I'm not saying that trip is a one-day or same-day thing. That, too, is inferred into FCR, though it is not accurate. FCR is not about time. Filter out the noise, and you will see the truth I'm trying to narrate here.

Allow me a story. Again.

As I am often wont to do, I relate my life and contact center strategies with food and dining experiences. There are few ways to tell a relatable tale than to describe a dining experience. Nearly everybody who would buy this book has been privileged enough to dine out at least once in their lives. Those who would not buy this book will be able to dine out even more. But as you dine out more and more, you start to get a bit picky about your food and the service. Hopefully the good reader is nodding their head in agreement, or at least finally accepting that the author is missing a few marbles.

Perhaps you can recall the chorus from the theme song of the long-running sitcom Cheers.

The Power of So

That's the spirit of it. That's the journey. It isn't a song about drinking a beer and going home. It's a song about where you will be while that happens. The journey. Now, here is the next story.

Having grown up in those lower economic segments, my family rarely went out to dinner. Sometimes at home, we ate mustard sandwiches because we had bread and mustard. As I grew up and my career started taking off, I made a promise to myself. My children wouldn't suffer that same boring sandwich experience or lack of reasonable options.

Imagine Scarlett O'Hara in Gone With the Wind, holding her fist to the sky as she proclaimed, "As God is my witness! As God is my witness, they're not going to lick me. I'm going to live through this, and when it's all over, I'll never be hungry again. No, nor any of my folk. If I have to lie, steal, cheat or kill. As God is my witness, I'll never be hungry again!"

I'm not nearly as attractive or skilled as Vivien Leigh was. I'm taller and maybe a bit pear-shaped with long, skinny legs. I can't act. Anyway, as I was saying, I made a promise to myself just as that literary character did. My children would experience the wondrous variety of foods out there. I would help them develop a palate and, as my Italian progeny, grow a profound fondness for great cuisine.

I may have also pumped my fist in the air or maybe dropped my game console controller onto my lap. But swear it, I did, and today my children have a very fair palate, and they have known very good food in their lives. At no point did they go hungry. I kept my promise.

At one of those moments in their young lives, there is one story where the meat of it really sticks out from all of this. Yes, the meat of it. Certainly not one of my proudest moments, as you will see.

This was a time when I was a single father. I took my four children to a local franchise of a prominent steak and salad bar chain. Again, not a proud moment, but it was close to home. They served a reasonable New York Strip that came with a loaded baked potato, and I could also get some veggies from the salad bar.

While this was no proper chop house, I was still quite hungry. I was anxious to bite into my steak. And I was nibbling on the rabbit food until the meat showed up.

Now, it takes an exceptional absence of talent to ruin a New York Strip. For those who have never worked a restaurant kitchen, there is this thing called "steak selection". Steak selection is all about picking the right cut of meat for the level of done-ness. A selection for a rare steak is vastly different than that for a tasteless and potentially carcinogenic well-done steak. As the chef or grill master, one must take special care when reviewing your refrigerated inventory for a steak targeted for medium-rare, rather than just reaching in a bin and grabbing the first thing you touch.

Well, the cook on this night was not so thoughtful. I sadly knew what was coming, and after waiting just a little bit too long to get our meals, my steak was served, and I instantly recognized that it was at least slightly overcooked. Because I was hungry (really, I was bordering hangry), I decided to just eat it as is.

Bad choice. Yes, I make many mistakes, it's true. Maybe that's for another book. I digress.

The steak was better selected for a well-done, leather-lover's steak. Gristle, too much fat, and certainly not medium rare, though they tried. That very thin strip of pink running horizontally through my steak was a dead giveaway. Cutting through the muscle was a workout. Chewing two bites was enough for me to tap out. My experience took a huge nosedive. They managed to ruin a New York Strip.

And then the service person disappeared for a little too long. My kids were eating. Their food was fair enough for them to continue. It takes an exceptional absence of talent to mess up... Never mind. Their food was acceptable. But our service person never came back to check. The seconds I waited felt like lots of individual and increasingly irritating seconds. They turned to minutes. No service person. Not even a floor manager. Nothing.

I took another stab at the salad bar to assuage my hunger. While I was eating my salad, the service person finally returned and asked how everything was. Quite directly, I described the inadequacies of my steak. Too long to be served, overcooked, and a poor selection. I advised the server to inform the kitchen that they should pay more attention to steak selection and proper preparation.

The server asked if I would like a new steak. I responded that I was fine and only wanted the message delivered to the kitchen. The server left our table, and we continued to eat. Note that at this point, I am still fine with the experience. I didn't walk in with my kids hoping for some kind of magical 4-star Michelin experience.

I also accept that stuff happens. We don't have to crucify or cancel a person because they made a mistake. We all live in glass houses. I'll be the first to raise my hand for that. "Mistakes are ok," I've always said to my children. "It's how we respond to the mistake that helps define who we are as humans."

Anyway, within perhaps two minutes, the server returned to our table with an empty plate and quickly jabbed a fork into my steak. She said, "I'll just take this back to the kitchen to show them what you mean. We'll get a new strip right out to you."

Meanwhile, I was staring at the space where my steak used to be. Instead of seeing an overcooked, tough steak, I saw green globules of congealed fat and broiler gunk. Even my sons, all three of them, said, "Ew, gross!" My daughter was still perhaps a bit young to process what we all saw.

I felt agitated...and ill. Having spent several years in the restaurant industry, I know what happens when the kitchen staff does not maintain a clean broiler or grill. In this case, it manifested as the aforementioned green globules of congealed fat and broiler gunk. I do not know if it is possible to say that enough before it no longer makes a person feel as if they need a shower.

I started wondering if I could finish my disastrous meal. Just then, the manager came to my table. (Note: This is the ONLY thing the server did right. Though it would have been entirely unnecessary had she just delivered my message to the kitchen staff!) The manager apologized profusely about my steak. He agreed that it was a poor selection and certainly not cooked properly. I was assured that the kitchen staff had been coached over the mistake, and my feedback was delivered.

I thanked the manager and stated that all I wanted was to ensure the kitchen staff got the message. That's all.

The manager then told me he was comping my meal.

"No need," I responded. I had two visits to the salad bar. I ate my potato. Those parts of the meal met my expectations. I can remember the challenges from my days in the restaurant business. Food cost. Very thin margins. I respect that. And so I restated that I only wanted to have my feedback given to the kitchen staff. The manager shook his head affirmatively, thanked me, and walked away.

As we were wrapping up our meal, the manager returned to our table with an envelope.

Let me pause at this point. Search the internet for a video clip titled It's Not About the Nail? Watch it. It's brilliant, succinct, entertaining, and relevant. Arguably the best 1 minute 41 seconds you will spend in your life if you simply pay attention, and I think everybody should watch and consider the story. There are so many lessons baked into this little clip. Now back to my story.

The manager began explaining to me that he was so sorry about my meal being unsatisfactory. He felt so bad, and while he recognized that I refused his offer to comp my meal, he decided to comp everybody's meal. In the envelope was the cash equivalent of the total bill for me and my kids. Being that there were five of us, there was close to $110 being given back to me.

I told the manager that his gesture, while kind, was entirely unnecessary. He insisted, thanked us for coming in, and expressed hope that we would return soon.

I. Was. Angry. On many levels, I was incensed. Let's list the reasons why.

1. The kitchen staff chose the wrong cut of meat.

- OK, it happens.

2. The kitchen staff cooked the meat incorrectly.

- Still OK. It happens.

3. The service person ignored my desire not to return the steak.

- Not OK. Listening is a fundamental element when seeking to deliver a great experience. Listen to your customer! And don't touch my food.

4. The broiler, apparently, was disturbingly dirty, and that grime was conveyed to my plate.

- Not OK, but maybe they were busy. Still not my problem, though. Don't serve me dirty food.

5. The manager ignored me. Completely.

- How many times must I say I only wanted my message conveyed to the kitchen staff? I'm tired of typing "kitchen staff". Imagine how off-put I was saying it out loud that many times!

- Also, don't make me repeat myself!
- OK, he didn't ignore me. He completely marginalized everything I had to say. That, in my mind, made his gesture entirely hollow.

Just as we see in It's Not About the Nail, the act of *just listening* is one of the greatest things we can do in the service delivery world or, frankly, if you want to display empathy and get closer to solving a problem in any part of life. I suppose it all depends on whose head has the nail, except both people must listen if positive progress is desired.

My point is that actively listening defines the foundation of each interaction or journey. It starts the experience in a positive manner. If the service person had listened to my request, none of this would have happened. If the manager had listened to my feedback, none of this would have escalated.

To wrap up the story, and to expose again my main personality flaw of hubris, I left the envelope on the table. Foolish? Egotistical? Stupid? Guilty on all counts. Though I felt I had to make my point, perhaps I should have just taken the money. I really hope the server understood why she got such a huge tip: I can be a real moron when it comes to making my point.

Except it was about service, not money. It wasn't even about the meal, per se. The service person and the manager tried to make the interaction all about resolving the cost of my meal. Their focus on resolution only served to make me never want to return. In focusing on resolution, they completely forgot to listen to me and seek to understand my concerns and feedback. Just as they ignored me, they ignored their responsibility to make each customer have a remarkable experience.

In the interest of setting up the next part of the story, I came in and ate a meal that I had ordered and paid for. That "service request" was completed. And it was a horrific experience handled poorly by the staff. The next story is how handling the experience properly changes the feelings at the resolution of the meal.

As I suggest in the chapter title, it is about the journey. In a dining scenario, it is about the service received and neither the cost nor the consumption of the meal.

When I apply this to a contact center environment, the support engineer listens, reads all the notes provided by the customer, and restates the issue in the engineer's own words. This shows active listening and is the gateway to a great experience, regardless of the resolution's details. In life, it is the same. Listen. Show me I'm important by listening to my concerns. Talk with me instead of to me. Repeat things I say. Speak my name often. Full stop. Great experience.

Now on to the next story. This part contrasts with the steakhouse story. In this story, I got a sandwich from Jimmy John's, a name most people can recognize. I love Jimmy John's sandwiches. Up to the time of this story, I never had a bad Jimmy John's experience. Never. For Pete's sake, I named one of my life lessons after Jimmy John's[7]!?

In this scenario, I was the Director of Support for a small company with exciting intellectual property. Our support team was small. Trying to juggle meal breaks was always a challenge. I had no idea that this day would spawn yet another lesson. Probably because I was busy, hungry, and not listening to the universe.

On this day, one of my team members asked to go on an early lunch to blow off some steam. I invited her to grab lunch for us, and I would pay. Even though Jimmy John's really does have fast delivery, we agreed it was best for her to make the trip to the restaurant and get out of our office for a few minutes. Being an effective thinker, she ordered online and went to pick up our lunches.

---

[7] Jimmy John's did not compensate me for this book or chapter. Nor do they endorse me or the way I write or think. Neither did I seek their permission to use them in my book, nor the repeated verbal deliveries of this lesson over time. I just freaking love Jimmy John's. If I ever go on a book tour, it would be nice if they would sponsor me and provide delicious, fresh sandwiches for everybody at every one of my stops. That might be like three or four sandwiches and a banner, and maybe some other stuff like chips or quartered pickles, but it would be really nice.

When she returned with our sandwiches, I opened the fine wrapping as if it were the most anticipated Christmas present of all time, only to discover that my #13 scarcely had a second piece of bread.

Eating this faux sandwich while wondering if it was actually an open-faced sandwich was quite a messy endeavor. I managed to get one half down before feeling inspired and in need of more napkins.

Fortunately, I took a picture before attempting to conquer whatever this was supposed to be.

I called the Jimmy John's manager and described my sandwich. I even offered to send her a picture. "No need," she said without missing a beat. "We clearly messed up and caused you to have a bad experience. Have lunch on us tomorrow. If it isn't the best Jimmy John's sandwich you've had, I'll even refund what you paid today."

Boom! Now, this is how you handle such matters. The manager acknowledged my concern, owned the mistake, and provided remediation that added extra accountability for her and her restaurant. While I'm generally fine with acknowledgement and ownership, I took her up on her offer. I rarely agree to replace food, but I wanted to see if she would follow through. Sometimes, this is precisely how I recruit valuable team members.

Anyway, the next day, that manager called me to see what time I wanted lunch (double bonus points!), and she sent a sandwich to my office at that time. It was every bit the Jimmy John's sandwich I have come to love...and expect. She listened, and she empathized, as great service evangelists will do. And with her focus on a great experience, she resolved my issue and created a memorable, positive experience along the way! And she kept my business.

Managing the experience is that important. Sure, I got my food. Placing the order was the service request. Eating the food was the resolution. But Jimmy John's managed the experience. They did that by listening to me, acknowledging my concern, and owning it, and they could have stopped there. But they set an expectation, which is a positive trigger for me. She described what to expect next and then delivered on that expectation.

No longer was I dwelling on the abomination of a fauxpen-faced sandwich. Instead, I was ecstatic at how well the Jimmy John's manager understood the journey! She could have walked away knowing that I received and ate my food. Issue resolved. Poor experience. Instead, she went the extra mile and made sure what lingered in my mind was how well she responded to my concern. That is what it's all about.

So how does this support this chapter's title, Service Over Resolution?

My contention is that we need to disrupt the norm and look directly at the customer. The customer's interpretation of the experience tells far more than how quickly the resolution was provided. Metrics like First Contact Resolution are nice, important, and precisely the wrong place to establish your core focus.

Instead, for the business world, create service cultures and values focused upon listening, teaming up with your customers, improving the service experience, and making customers feel as if they are important every single time! This will organically lead to resolution. Resolution is implicit in the creation of the service request. It will happen.

Focus on great service, and any concerns presented by the customer will be minimized. They, too, will focus on the service quality, and your customers will be as pleased as if they had just eaten a perfect Jimmy John's #13, freshly delivered.

Baron Davis:

Why aren't you the best?

"Some people want it to happen. Some wish it would happen. Others make it happen."

-Michael Jordan, Arguably the greatest basketball player of all time

Michael Jordan said it. There really are at least three different types of people. In the context of this chapter, I chose to focus on the same three flavors Jordan identifies.

Some people want it. These people are not generally content. You will hear them gripe about what someone owes them. Maybe they are like Uncle Rico in the brilliant movie Napoleon Dynamite. Having read chapters 7 and 8, you'll recognize that Uncle Rico hilariously overestimated his abilities and blamed the coach for keeping him off the playing field. There are two standout Uncle Rico quotes that demonstrate Uncle Rico didn't use the Craig Brown lesson and certainly didn't use the Gardening lesson.

"How much you wanna make a bet I can throw a football over them mountains?... Yeah... Coach woulda put me in the fourth quarter, we would've been state champions. No doubt. No doubt in my mind."

"Back in '82, I used to be able to toss a pigskin a quarter of a mile."

Not only is Uncle Rico a superb example of what happens without Craig Brown and Gardening, but he is also that disgruntled person who wants greatness but never worked for it. He is Jordan's "people who want it to happen."[8]

The next group, according to Jordan, is "Some wish it would happen." These people are closer to making it happen because of the power of the wish. I'm not saying wishes are a real thing in the real world. They aren't. Otherwise, my superpower would be dominion

---

[8] Let's not start with a third Uncle Rico quote of "Man I wish I could go back in time... I'd take state." Instead of being someone who "wishes it would happen," he is reflecting on the past. Rico is up to his neck in regret for which he believes he is not responsible. He is looking back and whinging about what already happened, instead of what he could do in the present. The wish he makes is that he could go back and take state. Maybe Jordan doesn't make that distinction, but I do.

Also, a mythological djinn would make a distinction here, too. No self-respecting djinn would grant a two-part wish of "go back" and "take state". Come on, people. I know someone went there when they read this. I'm only trying to head off the pointless arguments and djinn are some of the most unscrupulous, pedantic, intention-twisting beings of all time. Go back and take state? Where is back? Go? Take? And what exactly is state? As if. #djinnfacepalm.

over mosquitoes so I could vanquish my enemies. I'm not saying I have enemies, either. I just know some people who might deserve a few thousand itchy bites. No, that is not the kind of wish, nor the kind of reality I'm writing about.

Antoine de Saint-Exupéry, a French author and aviator, is credited with saying, "A goal without a plan is just a wish." That points right at the people who wish for something to happen. They see something they desire, possess, or accomplish, and they wish they were the person who did those things.

Rarely do these people actually plan out how to get what they want. They don't set actual goals. They see others doing something, living in luxury, hitting home runs, cloaked in fame, or whatever, and they dream about how it could be them. Perhaps they don't realize that they could possibly achieve those goals if they only made a plan. Or maybe they have a plan, but they haven't done the Craig Brown lesson or the Gardening lesson. Their goal becomes unachievable. Is doing something wrong with the intent of success the same as having a plan to achieve a goal that is out of reach?

Either way, these people fail to grasp the effort and mentality required to achieve the loftiest of their goals. They become a self-fulfilling prophecy of holding oneself just this side of greatness because they couldn't commit to the goals they may have made. Or perhaps they are too comfortable as the knighted champion of all things mediocre, and their wishes and plans are things they wrote down as if just that minimal effort were enough to earn their wishes. They just wished. How tragic is that?

Now for the last of Jordan's groups: "Others make it happen." These people have the vision, the intestinal fortitude, the drive, and the attitude to make it happen. Possibly this is you, but it is important to understand here that these things are not enough. The people who "make it happen" know this. Dreams to goals. Goals to plans. Choose to begin. The will to continue.

We can talk about these characteristics, and maybe you might say, "But MJ had skills!" And yes, he did! He was not born with those skills, though. Jordan wasn't born with a stronger drive or the guts to do what he did. No, Michael Jordan chose. And when he chose to do a thing, second best was not enough. Losing was unacceptable once he learned those lessons. He chose to keep going.

Because the real difference between someone like Michael Jordan and the rest of us is that he chose to make it happen. And that is how we come to one of my most favorite basketball players of all time: Baron Davis.

Though Davis may never be counted among the top point guards, there was a glimmering moment in time when it was impossible to argue that he was NBA Point Guard Royalty. He was drafted as the third pick in the 1999 NBA draft. That alone indicates the high expectations that were had by people in the know.

It took several years for Davis to find his cadence and place in the NBA as he fought through injuries and questionable coaching decisions. And then suddenly, Davis started causing serious damage over and over again against every team he played.

Eight years into the league, Davis went on an 11-game tear where he stuffed numbers in the box score at near-unheard-of rates. Davis averaged 25.3 points, 4.5 rebounds, 6.5 assists, and 2.91 steals in the postseason. This was probably the single greatest representation of Davis' potential.

But potential is all we could hope for.

In 2008, another second-tier point guard, Devin Harris, commented that Baron Davis was the best defender… when motivated. Harris said, "Baron is a major pain when he's motivated."

When he's motivated. And that seemed to be the way history and Davis' peers were to remember him.

Yet, one night years ago, I was watching Kenny "The Jet" Smith on the television. He was talking about great players of the time, and he mentioned an interaction with Baron Davis that resonated with me.

Smith related the story as follows:[9]

Smith: "On offense, is there anyone who can stop you?"

Davis: "No."

Smith: "On defense, is there anyone who can stop you?"

Davis: "No."

Smith, losing his shit: "Then why aren't you the best player on the court in every game?!"

And Smith meant it. Davis was really that good. When he wanted to be.

Now, I don't know Kenny Smith. I sadly don't know Baron Davis. But that interaction was powerful, and Smith asked a question that all of us should ask ourselves. We don't need to be in a pantheon of Point Guard Gods like Baron Davis before we get introspective. It doesn't even need to be about our chosen careers.

If you are passionate about something, shouldn't you strive to be the best in the game? Davis had what some might call a God-given talent. When he was in the game mentally, he could ball with the best. But he wasn't always passionate like, say, Jordan was. Taking nights off was not something in Jordan's lexicon.

---

[9] This is to the best of my recollection. I found only a couple of similar stories on the internet. They are essentially the same, but there are differences. My memory is that Smith asked Davis why he isn't the best on the court in every game.

But shouldn't we still aim high? Shouldn't we still take pride in what we do? Is it ever good enough to be the Defender of the Mediocre? This certainly isn't the time to invoke Mary Poppins', "Enough is as good as a feast." There is a time and place for that, but it is not here.

This is a time where you look at the work you do and ensure its quality speaks your name out loud. Otherwise, how can we ever talk about getting paid for what we do?

I take this interaction between Smith and Davis, and I share it with the team members who could best use it. Hopefully, you wondered why I wouldn't share it with all team members. I'm glad if you did have that thought.

When I think of basketball players, there are some great ones and some real stinkers. And the stinkers can still out-play most people on the planet. They have skills, much like the people on the teams I've managed. I contend the lesson is best used on the team members who will compete, who have the drive, and who are always seeking to improve. This lesson isn't for every team member.

The practiced leader will recognize that most team members do their job well enough. Enter Mary Poppins. We need those team members. They give us continuity through change and attrition. They are the people who will show up each day, follow our processes, do a good job, then go home to whatever they do after work. One might infer from normal distributions that this is about 68% of everybody…ish. That's not far off from reality.

Maybe some readers are a little incensed by that statement. Maybe some of you, like myself, have managed some really incredible teams. It's true. Stacked top to bottom. And maybe it's painful to suggest that one or two members of those really incredible teams weren't as good as the others.

I'm sorry, but that is just not realistic. To prove my point, I look to the single greatest collection of sporting talents in the history of competitive sports: the 1992 United States Olympic Dream Team.

This was a time when most every nation on the planet was sending their best professional players to the Olympics. It was clear that the US collegiate athletes were not competitive at the same level as many of the professionals from other countries. A decision was made to include professional athletes in the Olympic basketball team.

And it was a dream come true. Hyper-skilled, hyper-competitive athletes, the best in the game, all on the same team. Jordan and Pippen from the Bulls. Magic Johnson from the Lakers. Larry Bird from the Celtics. John Stockton and Karl Malone from the Jazz. Charles Barkley from the 76ers. Also there were greats like Patrick Ewing, David Robinson, Chris Mullin, Clyde Drexler, and Christian Laettner.

Arguably, these were the greatest NBA players on the planet, and Laettner had, at the time, one of the most prolific and successful careers in college basketball. And they took no prisoners. They won. It wasn't even close.

There were many discussions following the Dream Team's gold medal win that year. Among those discussions was one that sought to identify the best of those great players in the context of the Olympics. Let's consider some key statistics.

Charles Barkley led the Dream Team with 18 points per game. Karl Malone led in the rebounding category with 5.3 rebounds per game. Scottie Pippen led all US players with 5.9 assists per game. Laettner led in free throw percentage with .900. The 3-point leader was Barkley at .875, though Mullin hit more (14) than Barkley (7). Barkley also led in field goal percentage at .711. Arguably the greatest player of all time, Michael Jordan, did not lead the team in any single statistic.

What fun it was to debate who was the best of the best in the Olympics!

Until someone, me, asked, "But who was the worst?"

Nobody really wants to look at all these elite players and point to one, saying, "You were the least of these people!"

Nobody, that is, except me wanted to blueberry this thing.

No matter how you reasonably weight each metric performance category there is one player who comes out at the bottom. Playing only two games, this player missed all of his 3-point attempts. He had zero free throws. For points-rebounds-assists, he logged only 5-0.5-6. The next lowest player, Larry Bird, also logged two games, and had 9.5-3.5-1. Close, but no cigar. The lowest performing player, arguably, was the great John Stockton, who played very limited time due to having a broken tibia.

If I now bring this back to Baron Davis and asking only some team members why they aren't the best, you can see this is a matter of context. As a leader, we must be objective in measuring contributions and performance by each team member. We're asked to stack-rank our team members. Sometimes, that means putting great team members at the bottom.

Now why is this part of the conversation in a book about filters? This is for leaders and managing teams. It's about numbers and context. It's about seeking to understand, which is yet another chapter in this book.

During an interview, I was asked how I deal with the lowest performing team members on my team. I asked the interviewer what she meant by lowest performing. She replied, "Well, just that. Lowest performing."

"Hmmm," I sounded aloud. "That makes no sense to me at all. I need more context, because…" And I relayed to her my Dream Team story. I finished with describing to her that John Stockton was arguably the lowest performing team member because of a broken tibia.

I asked my interviewer, "If I were to turn the same question, absent clarification and context, on you, how would you answer it? And know that I don't expect you to give me an answer. I hope that my story teaches you how I would answer your question, and how I would view or define a 'lowest performer' on my teams."

She actually thanked me for the lesson and told me it would make her rethink how she poses that question in the future. I counted that as a leadership win. It is in this way that we guide our team members to be better, to bring their best game, to be their best selves. This is how we filter the noise when we grow and improve our team members.

Golf Lesson #1:

Redefine Success.

"And he that strives to touch the stars, Oft stumbles at a straw."

-Edmund Spencer

If you are like me, there are things you love to do, though most people prefer you would find different hobbies. I'm talking about things like golf, dancing, karaoke. Sure, I have a great time trying, and occasionally someone ends up in the hospital, but I have a good time!

For this particular rule, I will focus upon golf experiences and measuring the right things to gauge along the way in order to solve a problem. Solving the problem is not the end game. How the problem is solved matters so much more when we consider there is an "experience" factor involved.

Following is a real-life experience…as related to me by a friend. Yes, my friend actually had these experiences. Really.

A couple of friends were out golfing some time ago. Neither of these friends were close to pro, by any means. Bob had a single-digit handicap. Tevin's handicap might be best stated as physical.

This lesson is best described through the course of one hole in particular. A par 5 hole with a dogleg to the right, and bunkers strategically placed alongside the fairway and green to catch the golf balls of the daring, the foolish, and the amateur.

Bob teed up his ball. He measured the wind, noticed the bend of the fairway and the bunker placement. Bob picked his 3-wood, addressed the ball, and went through the precise motions of his well-practiced stroke.

The sound of contact with the ball can only be described as a "ting" that golfers of all competency levels recognize as the sound of tee-shot perfection. The sound resonated with the golfers' souls as they shaded the sun from their eyes and peered off into the distance. They saw the ball appear to track left, then slowly, gently lean back to the right to follow the curve of the fairway. They watched for the golf ball to land, bounce well over a bunker, roll, and come to a stop in what must be the perfect center of the fairway.

One stroke for Bob.

As Tevin's turn came up, he spoke in cocky, assured tones. Bob laughed at his false bravado. Bob understood what was about to happen and smiled at his friend anyway.

Tevin went through a similar routine. The ball was teed up, and Tevin had already selected his notorious driver, a club that cost more than Tevin's skill could justify. Nevertheless, the ball was addressed, the stroke concluded, and the resulting divot landed near the red tees.

Tevin's ball followed an entirely too flat trajectory for a short time. Then it cut an impossibly hard angle to the right, slicing off into the tall, unmanicured grass and rocks of the rough.

One stroke for Tevin.

Having secured the shortest drive, Tevin was up next. Finding his ball and lamenting the thickness of the surrounding grass and the less-than-optimal placement of the trees, Tevin opted to use his favorite 6-iron. Though not terribly practical for the situation, Tevin used his 6-iron for every uncertain stroke. And having addressed the ball, use it he did.

The iron was slowed by the grass, some of which Tevin uprooted in revenge.

Thankfully the clump of dirt, roots, and grass nearly went halfway as far as the ball. The ball managed to make it all the way to the first fairway bunker. To his chagrin, Tevin still was so far out as to have the next stroke.

Two strokes for Tevin.

With Tevin's next stroke, he used his sand wedge. His swing caused the foot of the clubhead to strike the ball just below mid-center. While the ball left the bunker, the trajectory was more akin to that of a bowling ball. The ball crossed the fairway and drew up just a few feet into the low rough. Best shot of the day so far. Laughter included.

Three strokes for Tevin.

Meanwhile, Bob took his second stroke from the fairway, where he had a straight shot between the bunkers, onto the green, and right at the flag. Bob used his 5-wood, took an easy swing, and watched his ball fly straight toward the green, bounce along the fairway, and roll to a stop about 15 feet from the green. It was another tremendous shot for Bob.

Two strokes for Bob.

Using his 6-iron once more, Tevin crushed his ball on the next swing. Impossibly straight, despite Tevin hoping to hit to the left of the bunker, the low rough still absorbed some of the impact, and the ball stopped just short of the bunker and stayed in the rough. The next shot was Tevin's.

Four strokes for Tevin.

If Tevin could identify the worst part of his golf game, he would say it is everything but putting. Tevin always was an optimist. Yet he tried to clear his mind and relax for the shot that could put him on the green. He took an easy stroke with his pitching wedge and his ball went surprisingly left. Missing the bunker he intended to shoot over, Tevin's ball rolled up on the green perhaps 35 feet from the pin.

Five strokes for Tevin.

Shocked to hear it was his turn, Bob selected a lap wedge and lined up near the ball. Two practice swings and he was ready. Bob addressed the ball, let out a slow, smooth breath, and swung. Everybody marveled at how oddly high Bob's ball went. Their wonderment grew as it landed eight feet from the pin, bounced twice, and rolled a few inches. He was maybe two feet from the hole. A certain gimme shot for Bob as he was on his way to a birdie.

Three strokes for Bob.

Tevin's next three putts finally put him one and a half feet from the hole. Suddenly, it was Bob's turn again.

Eight strokes for Tevin.

Bob humbly lined up his putter and took four easy, methodical practice swings, appearing more as a pendulum than a golfer. Without missing a beat, Bob stepped up to the ball, placing his putter behind it, and gently rolled the ball into the hole for birdie.

As they walked away from that hole, Bob recorded the scores. Bob finished with four strokes for birdie. Tevin finished with 10 frustrating strokes.

Perhaps all of us (except this author) have experienced this in life. But what are we really measuring?

In the world of golf, we measure strokes against a prescribed difficulty and expected number of drives, fairway shots, and two putts for every hole. In American football, we measure individual and team stats. In basketball, it is similar. And then in the end, everybody measures who crossed the finish line.

In this story, which was certainly conveyed to me by a friend, both golfers finished the task. One did it efficiently and effectively. The other... well, he was asked to never golf there again. But that's another story. From a friend. Anyway...

In life and in the business world, it is easy to focus on the finish line as a North Star guiding us in the right direction. That is typically good advice. But what if there is something different to measure? Something more about the experience, or something about the experience that gives us the opportunity to grow and improve along the way?

The real object lesson in this story is to look at how you measure success. Bob and Tevin both finished the hole. If finishing the hole is the measurement, Bob and Tevin are on equal ground. In golf, however, the measurement is the number of strokes. Clearly, Bob won in that sense.

Let's take a little detour.

What if your finish line is reaching a personal weight goal? That's the finish line. Every day, you weigh yourself in the morning. You go through your routine, which may include counting steps, a diet, or walking the dogs. But your eyes are on the finish line.

And every morning, your weight isn't changing.

This is an example of how finish lines are not the way to measure the experience. In the contact centers I have fixed, I often enter the landscape to find the company measures trailing, or lagging, metrics. To me, these are end-of-the-line metrics.

If I really want to lose weight, I don't weigh myself. I ask myself what I must do to lose weight. I look at the things I control. How much exercise, and what types, do I do? How many calories do I eat at each meal? What about my carbohydrate intake?

Now I'm moving away from the finish line and defining my success in different ways. I can change my dog walks to be longer and more frequent. That metric becomes something like Count of Walks > 1 Mile/Week. Another measurement can be limiting meals to 3 per day and only 700 calories per meal. (Note: Talk to a doctor. Know what your targets should be!) Or perhaps I could limit my carb intake by tragically reducing the number of pasta meals I eat in a day. Maybe that measurement is Moments of Fondly Honoring My Italian Heritage <= 1/week.

Now I have stopped focusing on the finish line and moved the spotlight to those events in between the start and the finish that really move the needle and improve the experience along the way to the finish line. While it's arguable that more pasta could improve the experience, I had to be honest to the spirit of this particular rule.

Let's bring this back to golf.

Clearly, Bob is the superior golfer. Tevin golfs for his own reasons and always finishes with some level of frustration. If Tevin wants to improve his golf experience, what can he do? If his finish line, his success, is decreasing strokes in 18 holes, he must redefine success into smaller, digestible steps that lead to that finish line.

There are many elements behind a good golf game, but let's start by leaving out the tools. Golf clubs are not directly part of the equation. Instead, we could focus on practicing at the driving range with each club. A metric could be something akin to X days at the range with the Driver, or maybe even more in the weeds with X balls hit per week with the Driver. How about completing three training videos or sessions focused on the Driver within three months?

When we get to this level, we can still track our handicap or perhaps our average strokes per 18 holes. We would expect that improving upon a single facet of the game will bring some level of lower strokes per 18 holes. But the focus isn't ever that far out. The focus is on the experience and the steps we take to get to the finish line.

Redefining the way we measure success is critical to preparing ourselves to work toward success. Often, we get caught up aiming and reaching for that star. And it is absolutely wonderful to keep and strive for lofty goals. But move your focus to the steps in between, and you will never trip on a simple straw.

The Other Golf Lesson:

Let it go.

"It's times like this my buddy Timon here says, 'You gotta put your behind in your past.'"

-Pumbaa, The Lion King

For those who pay attention, I use a lot of cinematic sources to share wisdom and insights. I'm always looking for relatable stories, movies, characters, activities, events, and such to build upon the rules and lessons I share with my mentees, team members, and peers.

I often use Mary Poppins as a source of Kevisms and wisdom. She was full of it. Wisdom, that is. Consider this: "A job well-begun is a job half done." Wow! Really, that is all kinds of WOW! Or this: "Enough is as good as a feast." Think well on that one. There are life lessons in this quote.

Yes, I love cinema for the characters, the writing, the storytelling... and yes, the quotes.

For this chapter's quote, and ultimately the purpose of the lesson, I use the underestimated boar from Disney's The Lion King, Pumbaa, as my source of applicable wisdom. Specifically, "You gotta put your behind in your past." Genius.

Unfortunately, this chapter is like a sequel to the last chapter. When I say "sequel," I don't mean something like the underrated Police Academy movies. I also don't suggest this is something like those brilliant documentaries about the life-long struggles of a young Italian boy who fled from Italy and arrived in the United States, only to amass a huge conglomeration of businesses with other Italian people. Nothing like that level of storytelling.

Neither is this some Greek tragedy like Highlander 2. I will not describe this abomination sequel if you promise never to watch it. Just watch the amazing first movie, Highlander, and then skip right to Highlander 3. Actually, skip right over that one, too. It was a bit entertaining, sure, but there are only perhaps two good lines in the whole movie. Just do yourself a favor. Don't watch those sequels.

For this sequel, it's more like the epically genius Kevin Smith's Clerks, Clerks 2, and Clerks 3. Many tragic events, a plethora of quotables, and humor so far out of the box that even the grotesque becomes hilarious. Who else could make a sentence like "Oh, cake!" possibly the funniest cinematic moment of all time? And in terms of cinematic dialogue, the power of those two words is exceeded only by the moment wherein the late, great Michael Nyqvist's Viggo Tarasov learns that his son, Iosef, had not only stolen John Wick's car but also killed his dog. Nyqvist's masterful delivery of the one-word sentence forever represents Nyqvist's character's moment of chilling fear, inescapable doom, and the realization that Iosef was inescapably going to die.

"Oh."

Yes, that's where this chapter goes. I must expose you again to the tragic golf story of the last chapter's hero, Tevin. Remember, Tevin is something like a friend of mine. I have observed his many experiences. His experiences often feed the lessons and rules I present in this book, be it due to his endeavors with golf, karaoke, dancing, or playing darts.

Oh.

Tevin loves golf, but mostly for the sunshine and the company. As I previously stated, Tevin's golf handicap had been inappropriately roasted as being physical. For the first half of Tevin's life, he golfed with irons his father gave him and a set of woods he bought from Sears. As with other tools of trade Tevin possessed, these were neither high quality nor made for his lanky frame and large hands. Had it been otherwise, and had Tevin received real, professional training, perhaps Tevin might have done fairly well at golf. The truth is, unfortunately, Tevin was just a shitty golfer. Tevin knew this.

The hole played out in the last chapter was quite typical for his game. It was common for Tevin to slice not just to the rough but sometimes more than halfway through the neighboring fairway. For those golf holes with a fence separating the course and a roadway, Tevin always tried to make unfortunate jokes about slicing into a passing car to cover up his lacking game. Tevin was sometimes a shitty person, too.

Tevin knew this as well.

Yet for reasons unknown to most psychiatrists Tevin had seen, Tevin rejected failure. Tevin had persisted in trying to improve his golf game in spite of the basics of the game being fundamentally out of his reach. He would hit more driving ranges, more rapid 9-hole rounds during a long lunch. Tevin even convinced his manager that he would come in for a shift at 6 am and work until 10 am, take a four-hour golf/lunch break until 2 pm, and finish the day at 6 pm. Yes, Tevin golfed five days weekly at that time. Indeed, Tevin was at the golf course in Midway, Utah, when his first son was about to be born.

Understanding this background is critical to grasping this rule. Hearing stories of Michael Jordan or Kobe Bryant and their competitiveness with everything they did, one may grasp part of Tevin's motivation. Competition. The drive to be the best in that moment, at whatever he was doing. Unwillingness to settle for less. Some people are born with it. Some of those people also have athletic abilities that elevate them well above their peers. And when you find someone who has that killer instinct, the obsession with being the best (or at least better than whomever you are with at that moment), with perhaps a slightly above-average athletic ability, you don't get Jordan or Bryant.

You get Tevin.

And Tevin never quits. Tevin's sin is hubris, but that's not the point right now. Tevin wants to win. Always. And so Tevin tries and tries and tries.

Often, that drive resulted in shanking balls into the water or the rough. More often than not, Tevin would lose an entire pack of balls through the completion of 18 holes. And now we can look back on the last chapter with some amount of context.

If you will remember, Tevin launched a flat, slicing rocket off to the right rough. He spent time carving his way out of the rough. At that point in his life, Tevin had spent more time trying to get out of the bunker sand than he tried getting onto a sandy beach. Topping off each hole with a horrible short game and a slightly less horrible putting. How frustrating it was to watch this play out.

Except Tevin never let it frustrate him. Long before Pumbaa said those oh-so-wise words, Tevin learned to let the last hole go. Tevin knew, as Pumbaa said, you gotta put your behind in your past. Forget the last hole. Sure, learn from it, but let all the frustration go.

Tevin recognized that if he was still thinking about his last drive slicing right, he couldn't focus properly on his next drive. Or even his next swing. Tevin learned to let it go so he could have better chances for success with his next attempt.

Now Tevin's golf game was not all that bad. Now and then, he would drop a 400-yard drive that came up just short of the green on a par 4. Tevin was notorious for the occasional clutch 30-foot putt. And sometimes, every once in a while, that 6-iron would make Tevin look like a magician of the links.

Tevin recognized, win or lose, he had the tools. If you have the tools and the drive, the only thing that can stop you is, well, you. And it is very easy to step on your own toes, get in your way, and even be your own worst enemy.

You know, Tevin's favorite sport was basketball. Due to a freakish growth spurt in his teens, it took some time to regain any hope of athletic coordination and capability. But work was needed, and work was done. Sadly, none of it came together until well into Tevin's 20s when, suddenly, he was a defensive beast on the court and could rattle off 30 points in a game with barely breaking a sweat.

Life interrupted Tevin just enough to remind him that his calling was elsewhere. After a handful of surgeries and a couple of children, it was clear that Tevin had to put his basketball behind him. Too little, too late, or so they say. And Tevin realized, embraced, the concept of letting it go. Learn as you will, but leave the last hole, the last game, behind you. Looking backwards turned out poorly for Lot in the Bible[10]. Probably it's a good enough maxim upon which I could build my lessons.

There are so many reasons to embrace this lesson in life, at work, or wherever.

When I use this lesson in the workplace, it is often done in the context of a contact center. Those people who have worked the phones are nodding their heads as they read here. Customers aren't always on the other end of the phone. Sometimes it is their shadow calling. You know what I mean. And that shadow says horrible things. Mean things. Evil things. In my contact center experiences, the shadow has threatened to kill my dogs. It has called my contact center minions horrible names that won't even come out of my well-skilled potty mouth. The shadow is there to murder your spirit and suck out all the joy of a job that is otherwise geared around serving our fellow humans. And there are more shadows out there than most people will acknowledge.

When I or my minions have received one of those many calls from the shadow, we always do our best to dance around the hate, remember our soft-skill torture trainings, create the best experience

---

[10] I have nothing against salt, mind you. Also, I do not wish to engage in a debate about the veracity of the Bible. I'm merely saying that unless you're backing up a very large vehicle through a crowded shopping mall, looking back is probably not a good philosophy in a figurative sense.

we can, and drive toward the implicit resolution with as little bloodshed or damage to our damnit-dolls as could be possible.

And what do I teach everybody to do next? Let it go. Put the last call behind you. Don't let it affect the next call. Don't let it ruin your day. The shadow used words and stuff. So? Move on. Remember your own joyful reasons for doing what you're doing, or for the people with whom you are doing these things.

If you let the shadow get in your head, it's like thinking about the tee shot you shanked into the rough. Or your battle in the bunker from which you are still getting sand out of your underwear six months later. When you carry the past with you, it never leaves, does it? Or is it better to say, you never let the past leave?

Pumbaa had it right. Put your behind in your past. Let the last hole...go. And then you can start again. With the next hole. With the next call. With the next investment. With the next relationship.

What Are You Trying To Solve: Filter Out The Noise.

"It's not information overload. It's filter failure."

-Clay Shirkey, American writer, consultant, and teacher of smart stuff

"Until you remove the noise, you're going to miss a lot of signal."

-Seth Godin, American author and ex-dot com executive

"The art of knowing is knowing what to ignore."

-Rumi, 13th century Persian poet, Islamic scholar, theologian, and Sufi mystic

This lesson is so crucial that it necessitates three important quotes. Three. Even if you may not know about the humans who wrote these things, you must examine them over and again until they are baked into your behavior.

In my long career, I have had the privilege of working with

some incredible humans, smart people, from whom I have managed to glean a significant volume of wisdom. I have had the good fortune of having an amazing mentor, for example.

My mentor was a career Chief Information Officer for many different companies. He had a global mentality and a singular focus on individuals. In one of the darkest times of my life, he supported me in a way my own father never did. All of these things were wonderful, but it was his singular focus that stuck with me.

It started with a small project engagement where I regularly used the word "server" to describe, for example, an SMTP mail server. While technically correct, our conversation led me to change it to system so that it would be understood globally. Little tiny change, that. Argumentative, yes. And it made me start asking more questions and looking outside my own fishbowl, as if drilling down to be more specific actually reveal more of everything.

I started applying this to my daily activities. This curiosity later became "blueberry the shit out of it." The abundance of relevant questions became "ask the right questions." Asking the right questions became "Seek to understand."

Problems unraveled in front of me. I was added to a project team that couldn't deliver on the definition and implementation of a change management process. The next day (yes, you read that right) I applied this lesson during my first project meeting. Assignments were made. Processes defined. The project delivered.

It concluded with our Chief Operating Officer, one of the greatest and most admirable humans I know, called me to his office and gave me perhaps the greatest compliment I have received.

"You have a talent for seeing through all the mud and the noise."

In other words, I solve problems. That's what I do.

Later, that same COO called me to his office yet again. I had submitted a solution for system access to our corporate directory services, using a development principle called privileged access. As my role was managing remote, independent offices in most of North America, and then rolling each office into a shared services model, I was keen to ensure that my remote IT Managers and Directors were rolled into that model without losing key access that allowed them to directly address local issues.

This was a contentious matter.

That last sentence was an understatement.

The central administrators wanted nobody to have any access at all. Nothing. Lock it down. That was fine. I understood. Yet, there was only the most negligible risk to assigning administrative access to location "containers". In my model, nobody except the central team had root access. Each container had an administrator who was in the office represented by the container.

The central team produced process and auditing. The remote admins could only execute activities in their own containers.

And then there I was in the COO's office.

He explained to me that while my recommendation appeared to be the correct way to go, the issue escalated to him and he couldn't be seen as always siding with me and my circle of influence, let's say.

I explained that all I did was provide the proper problem statement, which dealt with both system access and security, as well as remote team member involvement and remote office executive buy-in.

While politics won that day, it was acknowledged that I provided the right problem statement and solution. In business, sometimes posing such questions is not a win.

Fast forward a couple of years, and I was running a product and technical support center. I'll not name the company, nor people involved, but I can honestly say it was one of the three worst collections of leadership I had encountered at that point. That remains true today. I hate writing that, as they were good, well-intended people who, in my opinion, were simply caught up in the corporate cycle instead of solving problems.

It was in this environment that we had double-digit major incidents in one month. As this was a Software-as-a-Service offering, if one part of the system goes down, many of our customers go down. In some cases, our customers would lose tens of thousands of dollars if they filed certain reports late. Or if they had deadlines with the state or federal government, they could incur fines and penalties, as well. But most importantly, if the system didn't work, the customers couldn't sell their goods and services. At all. Some of these customers did millions of dollars in sales daily across their family of "stores".

So one major incident is bad. Two is terrible. Thirteen is shutting down the company for nearly half a month. And when the system didn't work as expected, the customers called me and my team.

As you might expect, our live call volume increased quite dramatically. In one particular month, the call volume rose over 35% due to the number of major incidents. Our executive team was justifiably upset at our quarterly business review.

And it was my turn to deliver the support center's quarterly performance report.

As I described the increased call volume and correlated it to the major incidents, well... Let's say that is when a sizeable volume of human waste was projected violently and directly at the air circulation mechanism.

I started an argument of epic proportions. My GM was upset. The CIO was upset. The CEO was confused. My own VP just kept saying, "Yes, that did happen."

I was excused from the room, but with two tasks. First, prove there were actually that many major incidents. Second, show the correlation of call volume with the dates of the incidents.

The GM tried to calm the room and the conversation that came out with all the attendees. He was spinning the situation as actually a failure on the contact center to return calls. There was no problem with the system.

As I worked through this with my then-VP, I thought back to my mentor. I thought about his guidance and his focus. I coughed up a question: "What are we trying to solve here?"

We had data already that showed the correlation of major incidents to increased daily volume. We could show it down to the minute. Yet it was regularly refuted by the GM, as he sent exactly the same data to the CEO.

I kept asking that same question. What are we trying to solve?

There was so much noise. Finger-pointing and threats in every direction. Explains this and explain that. Why are these tickets codified this way? What are you teaching your department? Let's remove the "Left Customer Message" status on our tickets! Yes, the GM's solution was to eliminate our codification method demonstrating we had called the customer back so that he could claim we had not called the customer back. Forget that we had call logs for correlation.

Let me tell you, I've been to concerts. I was in the pit for Van Halen and Bon Jovi. You need earplugs for Poison. Aerosmith jams. Skid Row, Faster Pussycat, Def Leppard, Motley Crue, Warrant...I did the rounds with the hair metal bands of the 80s. I've squeaked out a fart in a packed elevator. I know all too well what noise is.

Noise is every argument, every sentence, each sound of frustration that is made to distract you from your course. You might consider them the logical fallacy known as a red herring. You wouldn't be wrong.

The purpose of noise is to distract you from what you are trying to solve.

Look back now at the quotes for this chapter and consider how powerful and important they are. There are three because all three are so impactful and have perhaps a slightly different view of the point of this lesson.

Clay Shirky suggested that if there is so much noise, you are failing to filter it out. You are not focused. You are not solving the problem. Perhaps you cannot even describe what it is you are actually trying to solve because there is so much noise you are letting in!

Seth Godin rightly instructs us that you will miss the point if you don't eliminate the noise. These red herrings will drag you in every direction except where you need to be going.

Rumi put it much more succinctly. "The art of knowing is knowing what to ignore." In other words, if you want to find answers, you have to filter out the distractions, and you have to focus.

Just as I gleaned from my mentor. Focus.

My question: What are you trying to solve?

The question had nothing to do with team training. The data were clear and consistent. The question had nothing to do with codification. Example after example showed that customers were calling for status updates, and not follow-ups to previous, unrelated issues. It certainly had nothing to do with a status that showed we had left voice messages with the customers at specific times on specific dates.

Red herring after red herring. And what were we trying to solve?

The question had nothing to do with team training. The data were clear and consistent. The question had nothing to do with codification. Example after example showed that customers were calling for status updates, and not follow-ups to previous, unrelated issues. It certainly had nothing to do with a status that showed we had left voice messages with the customers at specific times on specific dates.

Red herring after red herring. And what were we trying to solve?

I stood my ground. I presented the data again, showing the correlations, showing the content, and arriving at the same conclusion. When we have 13 major incidents in one month, customers get pissed off and call the contact center more often.

The assertion of my own question was presented again. I indicated that the problem statement was that "when the system is down, customers call more." If we are concerned about anomalous call volume (e.g. a month where volume increases more than 35% then drops back down to normal volumes the next month) then identify the cause of the calls.

If the calls are strongly correlated to the major incidents, fix the major incidents. Find out why we have those incidents. Honestly, those causes were known, but there was an irrational rejection of cause and effect.

This is an odd story to tell in an effort to teach a lesson. The entire conflict didn't end well for a few people, including myself…though "end well" is subjective. It's easy enough to ask, "What are we solving?" and then point in a direction. That's not it. If you're still thinking that's all there is to it, I'm failing.

I once interviewed a gentleman in my office. He was applying for a technical support role, and I was the hiring manager. As we did our back-and-forth, we consumed the scheduled time. As I closed out the interview, I asked if he had any further questions for me. He did.

"Yeah," he replied. "What are those?" He pointed to my whiteboard where, in blue dry-erase marker, I had written my list of rules and lessons. As you've seen in this book, some of the chapter names are, well, odd. They caught his eye, and he was curious.

My blueberry gong sounded. In my internal Darth Vader monolog voice, I thought, Yes, the Force is strong with this one! I asked him to pick only one and I would explain it to him. He picked the lesson titled "What are you trying to solve?" The purpose behind this chapter.

I explained the lesson to him, how it ties into other lessons, but ultimately it is about filtering out the noise and focusing on the real problem.

He really liked what I described. In a bit of a solemn awe-struck tone, he said to me, "Nobody teaches that. Nobody. Not where I work. I've never had anybody teach me that."

After my interviews were complete, I hired this gentleman along with one other candidate. It was his second or third day on the job when he came to my office and leaned against the doorway.

He said, "You know, that lesson we talked about in my interview was amazing!" He continued on with describing an argument he had with his wife the previous weekend. It was going nowhere. Then he remembered our conversation and this rule.

He asked his wife, "What are we trying to solve?"

As he finished the story, he told me that asking that question out loud absolutely stopped the argument. His wife told him what she thought the problem was. He told her what he thought the problem was. They were able to then work together to sort things out. They filtered the noise. They learned how to ignore what needed to be ignored. They cleared out the noise enough that they got each other's signal.

Shirkey, Godin, and Rumi. I don't know any of them. All of them are or were important humans. They had something to share. Rumi is long gone, but maybe one day Mr. Shirkey and Mr. Godin will say something about some lunatic career contact center leader and how he helped people understand what they said. When that day comes, I'll be fingerpainting in my office.

It's Not Done Until It's Done:

Fix your outbound filter, too!

"Are we there yet?"

-Children, since travel was invented.

"Close only counts in horseshoes and hand grenades."

-Frank Robinson

"Let's not be so quick to dismiss nuclear warfare in that conversation."

-Kev

Words matter. This is something certain recent world leaders, or a specific former world leader, failed to realize.

When you have a position of power and you speak words, those words have an impact. They mean something. People make decisions based upon those words. As your position and power are greater, so is the meaning and impact of those words.

Case in point: Donald J. Trump, former President of the United States. Though he was no infectious disease doctor or scientist, his words propelled the pharmaceutical drug hydroxychloroquine for off-label use in combating the COVID-19 virus without any evidence for efficacy. People died as a result of their attempts to use hydroxychloroquine to fight that virus. Words matter.

Later, a Trump ally, Rudolph "Rudy" Giuliani, accused, without evidence or through the misrepresentation of evidence, two poll workers of mishandling ballots. Giuliani spread his misinformation far and wide, even to the point that his two targets received death threats, lost their jobs, had to relocate. Their lives were uprooted. Later, in 2023, Giuliani was held accountable for his words to the tune of $148 million dollars in damages awarded to the two poll workers. Words matter.

Again, I've used extreme examples to capture the spirit of this rule. It's not done until it's done. How is this important in terms of filtering?

One must be specific, precise, and accurate.

Sometimes, the noise that must be filtered is that noise coming forth from our own gray matter. Our own mouths. We must discipline ourselves not only to tune out the noise from the outside but the noise from within as well.

This manifests as a pet peeve of mine. It's not done until it's done.

Usually, we might see this as the ubiquitous comment, "Almost done!" What the hell is that?

I'm reminded of a scene from what is arguably the greatest movie of all time: The Princess Bride. Some readers already know the scene.

"Your friend here is only *mostly dead*," Miracle Max explains to Inigo Montoya. Words matter. Westley is not dead. He is not done. He is only *mostly* done.

This is great news for our heroes and our story. In the world of business, it usually doesn't end up that way, unfortunately.

The typical conversation might go like this:

Project Manager Alice: "Hey Bob, that system build is due today at noon. It's 11am. Where are we right now?"

Bob: "Oh yeah. I'm nearly done with that. A few more minutes, Alice."

The ambiguity is amorphous and should frighten any seasoned project manager. Well, maybe not frighten. A reasonable PM knows what to do. Let's change the scenario a bit.

Captain Alice: "Sergeant Bob, have you finished aborting the nuclear bomb launch?"

Sergeant Bob: "Yes ma'am, I'm almost done, Capt. Alice. Almost done. Don't you worry."

Or this example:

Submarine Captain Bob: "Chief Alice, have you secured the hatch? We're ready to dive!"

Chief Alice: "Yes sir, almost done!"

These words change the direction of the next step. The answer both times should have been "NO!" Why? Because done is a binary measure. Think of it that way, and that is why I use done as the trigger for this filtering concept.

When Chief Alice responds with "Yes sir, almost done!" she contradicts her own answer. She causes confusion. Which is it? Yes or almost done? Why differentiate? Because "almost done" is the opposite of "done". Indeed, "almost done" is literally "not done".

Thus, the title of the chapter, "It's not done until it's done." I'm just trying to keep you all honest and make your filters work both ways!

And this one takes more discipline. It upsets people, too. Truly.

I'll be honest, I abuse this rule. A lot. People get offended. Why? Because so many people have a broken outbound filter.

There are no stupid people, just stupid questions. Isn't that how the old saying goes? If that isn't it, that's how it should be.

And it's silly things, too. It starts simple and gets worse.

"Can I ask you a question?" Sigh. Now this is being very pedantic. Like I said earlier, it's a pet peeve. It is. And I like to solve problems. When I solve problems, clear a path. Let me get to doing what I do best. This book is about filtering out the noise, bringing about a clarity of thought, focusing, precision. To ask that of people around us, we must provide the same.

And so the words coming forth from our mouths must necessarily provide the same respect to our listeners and partners as we expect from them. Therefore, we never offer up the equivalent of "It's almost done."

We change our behavior to filter out such imprecise noise. Be that in our estimates, our calculations, or what have you. This breeds, again, a certain level of pedantry. I contend that when filtering out distractions and noise, this precision in communication carries enormous value.

Let's look again at our examples in this new light.

Project Manager Alice: "Hey Bob, that system build is due today at noon. It's 11am. Where are we right now?"

Bob: "I am not done, Alice. I require another 40 minutes to complete my task. I will contact you with an update at 11:40 regardless of my status."

There is no ambiguity. The task is incomplete, yet Bob has

set a time expectation and another expectation for his next update. Alice knows that the update will come at 11:40 and will have a small amount of time left before the task is due. She can make decisions in that remaining hour to help Bob or accept the risk that Bob's estimate works for the project. Here is the other example.

> Capt. Alice: "Sgt. Bob, have you finished aborting the nuclear bomb launch?"

> Sgt. Bob: "No, Capt. Alice. I have five more steps to follow according to the documented process. It should take me two more minutes. I will alert you on my completion or if I run into any complications."

Capt. Alice now knows precisely where she stands in this critical process and can make any decision that is appropriate in the scenario.

Or this example:

> Submarine Capt. Bob: "Chief Alice, have you secured the hatch? We're ready to dive!"

> Chief Alice: "No, sir! We need 30 seconds more."

Clear and precise. We are not done. Do not dive if you love this sub and the people aboard. Easy to make decisions with that information, right? This is what filters do for us. Less noise, easier to make decisions. This is why I wrote this book, for crying into another filter very quietly.

The point is filters are a two-way street. While most of the filtering we focus on is external, do not forget that part of the discipline or baking-in that we must achieve is to control our outbound filter, too. Offer up a level of precision that contributes to the filtered, noiseless environment in which we seek to solve those complex problems most efficiently.

This is our gift to the world. It is not done until it's done.

Seek to Understand:

Another way to filter noise.

"Instead of seeking to pinpoint blame, seek to understand cause."

-Neale Donald Walsch

"Seek to understand the problem in front of you. If you understand the problem, you have taken the first step toward solving the problem."

-Kev

You, the reader, probably have not read this in my writings before, but I'm here to tell you this may be the single most important lesson I evangelize. It's true. Seek to understand. It is one of the greatest approaches to filtering out the noise. Bake this one into your behaviors, be that for life in general, leadership, problem solving, or what have you.

Far too often, both in life and the workplace, I've experienced people who rush headfirst into problems without seeking to understand. I have shared in a previous chapter a situation where multiple system incidents caused a 35% increase in call volume. Executive management failed to ask the right questions in an epic example of not seeking to understand the real problem.

If you don't seek to understand the problem in front of you, how in the world can you solve that problem?

For married couples or people in a relationship, when having a conflict, there is no resolution if both parties cannot agree upon what the problem is. That problem cannot be agreed upon without earnestly seeking to understand the grievance your partner is attempting to present.

Seek to understand.

Here I will share a troubling experience I had with a doctor. Let me say from a perspective of caution, I understand why a doctor would take the position this doctor took. However, the doctor in question did not present his position in this manner.

And so for nearly five months of my life, I carried over my head the dark cloud of a cancer diagnosis while awaiting various specialist appointments and test results. Why? Because my new general practitioner would not put all the data in front of him, listen to the information I wanted to share, and ultimately, seek to understand.

I know that I am not the medical professional in this story. I don't wish to inflict the scenario with my hubris. Indeed, you will see at the end of the story, even the specialist agreed with my own assessment. So please, don't stop here and say to yourself, "This Kev guy has a real ego problem trying to out-diagnose an experienced doctor." That's not the case. Read on.

For much of my adult life, I have had sleep apnea. This affliction has a great deal of long-term impact on a person's health, and I won't go into much of that here. It suffices to say it can complicate weight problems and various aspects of men's health such as the production of testosterone, both of which are germane to this story. Both problems feed on each other like a cruel cycle.

Here I was, a man in my mid-40s, and my GP had just retired. I was searching for a new doctor and had settled on a reputable professional near my home. I scheduled my first appointment and informed the receptionist there would be a lengthy discussion to bring the doctor up to speed on the health issues I had been dealing with.

At the same time, I was making weekly visits to a local men's health clinic with another trusted medical professional to deal with the diminished testosterone production.[11] The output of this treatment

---

[11] Listen up, humans who both depend upon testosterone production AND are subject to getting older: I am not a doctor. Seek professional medical advice on

was amazing and powerful. Perhaps a bit too much, though.

Side effects of testosterone therapy include higher production of estrogen and red blood cells. From my experience, there is some advice I must impart.

First, always discuss what you feel with your doctor. Second, don't watch movies like The Notebook, What Dreams May Come, or any clips of Roy Firestone interviewing professional athletes. You will weep like a child who just discovered that mom and dad just ate all their Halloween candy. And certain specific regions of your chest will ache. I can't say this part is bad, but it's awfully distracting.

Third, this is where the red blood cell production comes in. It's potentially harmful. The professionals who administer the testosterone therapy must have a protocol for regularly testing your red blood cell count. When it reaches a certain level, action must be taken. To my surprise, that action was, as I called it, leeching.

Yes, I was stabbed with a needle, connected to a tube, and

---

this topic. As you age, at a certain point, your testosterone production slows down. It's normal. And you do not have to accept it as ok. You can get treatment. You can exercise! You can alter your diet! It is an amazing feeling. You do not have to feel old and tired and weak. Talk with a doctor about this and get tested regularly. Seek to understand this problem, too!

drained into a bag. They leeched off my blood into a bag because my red blood cell count went too high. It felt like a very medieval thing to do. [12]

The short of it is that an increased red blood cell count is inevitable, much like Thanos when undergoing testosterone therapy.

Switch back now to my new GP and my first visit where I'm discussing my long list of health issues. I get to the point where I mention the intersection of a few things, including sleep apnea, low testosterone count, testosterone therapy, and I make certain to mention the known side effects, etc. To wit, you will see x, y, and z. Do not worry.

Why do I highlight this specifically? Because in this context, $x + y + z$ = polycythemia vera. And that may also be diagnosed as blood cancer. Except if I use my sleep apnea equipment regularly and don't use testosterone therapy, etc., I don't have x, y, and z. Therefore, as I explained to the doctor, I don't have polycythemia vera.

The doctor, being a good doctor, wanted to do the leg work himself. I understood, and we did the blood work. I felt that I had ably and amply informed him. He was armed with information.

---

[12] Also, write off donating blood if you are on testosterone therapy. Apparently, drug users will do t-therapy to cover up something or other. If you tell the Red Cross people you're doing therapy, they will cancel you!

The following Monday, I received a call from his office and was asked to come in immediately. They couldn't tell me why. That's always bad. So I made arrangements and arrived at the office anticipating some kind of bad news.

Finally, I was face to face with the good doctor, and he got right down to business.

"Kev, you have cancer," he declared. "I'm referring you to the local cancer clinic at the hospital. When I reviewed your blood panel, your red blood cell count is way too high. You have what is called polycythemia vera, or PV. It's a type of blood cancer."

I replied to him, a bit perturbed, "But do you remember from our discussion last week that I'm on testosterone therapy and I have sleep apnea? Both of those amplify my red blood cell production. I just need to be leeched a bit more. I am fine, and I don't have cancer."

With a small sigh, the doctor said, "It's quite common to be in denial with a diagnosis like this. I know this is only our second visit, so not a lot of trust is built yet. I'm confident of the diagnosis. I wouldn't direct you to a cancer clinic if I weren't certain, Kevin. This is the next step. You have cancer."

Again, I understand from this doctor's perspective that he had facts that must be dealt with. He had context, rules, and such. He couldn't say this fit in the definition of cancer and not do something about it. Malpractice, right?

From my perspective, I couldn't understand why the underlying information couldn't be applied to the situation. Knowing that I couldn't win a debate on the doctor's territory, I accepted his decision, and his staff made arrangements for me to go to the cancer clinic.

It took almost four bloody months to get into the specialist. Imagine living under the cloud of "you have cancer" for that long. Not "you might have cancer." No, that doctor was clear to me. "I'm confident of the diagnosis," he had said. I had cancer. And cancer means you're dying. It took my father and my maternal grandmother.

Cancer means death. I went into a deep depression in those nearly four months.

I finally got to meet with the cancer specialist. He reviewed my blood work, and I explained the same $x + y + z$ thing to him. His response?

"Absolutely. That's common knowledge. I'm glad you're informed on the treatment you're getting. In fact, I'm disturbed that your doctor was informed of this and still sent you here. The blood work combined with this information doesn't even justify this visit. It's a waste of time, and you've been going how long thinking you've got cancer? I'm really sorry! But let's not waste the moment.

I can run a DNA test just to make sure. Maybe your doctor doesn't know about this. It's a little pricey, and your insurance doesn't cover it. But it will definitively inform us if you have PV or not. The results will take a few weeks, but we will know."

I wanted to break down and weep. I felt vindicated, sure, but the relief of not having that death sentence hanging over me was just indescribable. And that power of the specialist in his own way saying, "let's seek to understand the truth of the matter," carried so much positive energy for me. I happily and eagerly paid for the DNA test.

One month later, the results showed that I never had cancer. I got a new doctor.

Seek to understand.

Now I was also able to filter out the noise that stopped me from understanding or that was unwilling to seek understanding. That was a side benefit of the exercise. I do not intend to disparage the GP at all. Again, I understand the conundrum he was in. What would I have done if I had his same training and experience? I can't say, but I moved on, and I'm quite happy with my next new doctor.

I hope this extreme situation paints a picture of the importance of seeking to understand. The curse of cancer is a grievous, brutal thing to carry for almost four months. I watched it kill my father in 2001. I was a teen when it took my mother's mother. My second son is a cancer survivor, though that came after my own experience. He went from not feeling right on Wednesday to a cancer survivor on Friday. Cancer is evil. I yearn for the day when we teach about cancer only in history classes.

Having read this far into this book, one might be thinking something like, "Isn't this about the same thing as 'Ask the right questions'?" Or if you read ahead, perhaps it is like 'The blueberry lesson'.

I submit that these are part of the aforementioned pattern. Not exactly the same thing, but rather complementary to one another. Ask the right question, seek to understand, blueberry (look inside!)

Bake into your behaviors these patterns, and the noise remains outside. Your filters become powerful. Problem-solving becomes second nature.

The Blueberry Lesson:

Be curious about everything.

"I have no special talent. I am only passionately curious."

-Albert Einstein, world renowned failure at math, but good at other stuff

"Blueberry the shit out of that thing!"

-Kev

The blueberry lesson is a personal favorite of mine, and I owe this to the single greatest entrepreneurial mind I have ever encountered. If you ran into Kim today and asked her about me, her response might be something like, "That sonofabitch? What is he up to these days?"

I really need to call her. We worked together for less than a year. She had been a Novell VAR in Novell's heyday. If memory serves, she was the largest VAR in the Midwest. If you had worked in Novell's partner channels, you would know that your success was not due to Novell. And because of that, Novell went from a >80% market share in networked file and print services to a footnote in the history of high tech.

Poor leadership, no real marketing, and a sales strategy that simply insisted you sign on the dotted line. All of this was happening while their only legitimate competitor, Microsoft, was throwing free CDs around full of software like Exchange, their business productivity tools that played a distant 2nd to WordPerfect's suite of tools, and an operating system called Windows NT.

The rest is history. In spite of Novell's merg...er...acquisition of WordPerfect, Novell could only find use for the former WP GroupWise product, and they couldn't compete with Microsoft's marketing and flood of free software that made NT, Word, Excel, and such, ubiquitous in the workplace. Then MS marketed this funky "integration" concept, and a lack of understanding cemented Microsoft's place in computing history.

I digress. The point is that Novell abandoned their VAR channel and faded away. Kim, being the person she was, persisted on sheer will, and that entrepreneurial mentality that causes one to vomit great business ideas like a college freshman fraternity pledge vomits chow mein from the all-you-can-eat Chinese Buffet at their fraternity's tequila meet-and-greet later that night.

In other words, it starts out ok, gets a bit messy, you filter out a bunch of the noise, and somehow you find an unchewed piece of shrimp or two in there. I don't know. Sometimes metaphors fail me. Anyway, with Kim, this was a daily thing. Ideas, not vomiting.

It seemed the conversation could be on any topic, and she would suddenly take notes, or tell someone to do something about whatever.

Never with Kim's ideas were there considerations for how we would get things done, or how much it would cost, or how many people were needed to make it happen. She was the idea person, and she was great at it. Don't bother her with the details. The details were my job, or whichever leader was nearby enough to own something else.

One day, Kim turned the tables on me. After explaining that I'm a guy who fixes what's broken, she informed me that today was different. She wanted me to cough up an idea that my dev team would produce and put to market within a year. I stewed on it for a bit, then told her the buzzword of the day was ITIL. Yeah, this was a while ago. I also mentioned that the ASP model of hosting had evolved to something they called Software as a Service. My entrepreneurial idea was to host a multi-tenant system for the core elements of IT Service Management and ITIL. It started with asset management, incident management, problem management, and a little more. I was quite proud of the idea, though we never started it. [13]

____

[13] See also the incredible company and their flagship (no pun intended) offering, ServiceNow. Founded one year before I thought I had this incredible idea…

Kim told me to make it happen. I was stunned. We were already on the threshold of delivering my first poor taste of a minimally viable product for her company, and that was being done by working my team of developers 90 hours weekly as we approached the go-live. I was borrowing developers from her consulting branch of the business. These guys were the revenue generators of the company. So they had to work at least 40 hours for their assigned accounts, and then they were authorized to put in another 20-30 hours for my project. In my experience, this is how entrepreneurs are.

Anyway, we delivered the first product. It was a Flash-based replacement of their legacy yacht-race tracking system. We were fixing bugs and updating our client build hourly on the morning of the Tracker's inaugural race, the Chi-Mac that runs north out of Chicago harbor to around the tip of the Michigan glove where Mackinaw Island is found. Though we were hot fixing bugs, the product was well received by the families of the yacht crews.

Kim sailed her own boat, Ozymandias IV, and so I had no contact with her until several days later when she and her crew crossed the finish line. To keep the story short, good job getting the new client out, why are you still fixing bugs, and where is this ITIL thing? Kim was an extraordinary entrepreneur.

I tell that story to start another. One evening after working very late, Kim offered to take me and one of our other Directors to dinner, but we would be with a client, too. It was a blast. The social side of Kim was unequalled in my book. She had no filter, and after a few minutes, you are glad for that between the belly laughs. Yes, Kim was an entrepreneur. And Kim was also a sailor.

And on that night she asked me a question I've never been able to shake from my head until I incorporated it into my growing set of rules and lessons. The same upon which this chapter is based. What was that life-changing, earth-shaking question?

"Kevin," she asked, "what color is the inside of a blueberry grown in Germany?"

In one of the rarest of moments in my life, I opened my mouth to say something, yet our eyes met and no sound came from my entire being. German blueberries? I freaking love blueberries. Indeed, blueberries are hands-down my most favorite fruit. I literally eat about a pound a day of those little, round, delicious, balls of happiness. In all of my life, however, blueberries served their purpose as I consumed them whole. I never looked inside. That, I thought, was not the blueberry's purpose. And so I responded.

"German blueberries? What does it matter when the purpose of the blueberry is to be eaten?" Such was a philosophy I designed through my life. As long as purpose is satisfied, nothing else matters.

It resonated with me when in the movie Speed, Dennis Hopper's Howard Payne explains to Keanu Reeve's Jack Traven that Jack is getting in the way for the wrong reasons.

"A bomb is made to explode," Payne explained. "That's its meaning. It's purpose! Your life is empty because you spend it trying to stop the bomb from...becoming."

It made sense to me in 1994, anyway. And what else is a blueberry good for if it isn't to be eaten?

Kim replied to me, "Kevin, that's your problem. You think you have answers, but you haven't even done something so simple as to look at what's inside a goddamn blueberry."

I immediately recognized that I was getting coached, or rather that Kim was presenting a moment I could use as being coached. If I had horse ears, they would have been fixed squarely on Kim's face. She had my full attention.

Kim went on to explain that a little bit of curiosity is what can take a good person to a great level. Sometimes she had referred to it as fault testing. Kim's definition of software fault testing included jerking your mouse around while holding down certain various keys. Dig around. Do stupid shit. Do things that don't make sense. Discover and learn. It sounded silly then, but I was being schooled most epically and expertly.

Look inside a blueberry when you're eating them. Once you have bitten halfway through a blueberry grown in Germany, tell me what you learned! This was her lesson. But it wasn't about blueberries, per se. Nor was it about doing untold things with your computer's mouse. No, it was about just open your eyes, observe, inquire, be curious, and don't settle for surface answers that feel adequate.

What was it I responded with? Oh yes, "What does it matter when the purpose of the blueberry is to be eaten?" No truer words have been spoken, but did that mean I had reached the end of all truths?

No.

Today, as I mentioned earlier, I eat nearly a pound of blueberries daily. I love blueberries. There are only so many items on my favorite foods list. The first five items on that list, in no particular order, are molasses cookies, authentic Italian pasta dishes (though if pressed for one specific dish, cacio e pepe), a stadium dog with mustard, a proper bread and butter pudding with raisins (find the recipe from former royal chef, Darren McGrady, and then prepare to speak with your clergy), and...blueberries.

I grab molasses cookies whenever I see them on the shelf, and I've only met one person who would make them for me. We're no longer married, so the odds of getting the good stuff are next to zero.

I make cacio maybe once every couple of months. Sometimes I'll rotate in a 3-ingredient spaghetti (Marcella Hazan's own recipe), aglio e olio, or a pasta with browned butter and mizithra cheese, but cacio is the favorite for me.

After Covid-19 and I haven't been in such a public place as a stadium. I tried the next best thing, a Costco dog, and found that those bad boys, delicious as they are, cause me...problems, let's say. I may need to change my list.

I've made the bread and butter pudding a few times. One may sin only so much in a single life. Especially when the good doctor advises watching my weight, cutting carbs, and stop eating all things good and wonderful on this earth. Perhaps if 2024 goes well, I'll commit another sin. Just because it is a favorite or a top 5, it doesn't mean I eat it often or even every day.

Except for blueberries. I eat almost a pound of blueberries daily during the blueberry season.

I'll sit at the table each morning, and my granddaughter joins me. Both of us mindlessly move blueberries from bowl to mouth like a couple of automatons processing today's produce. She draws, and I read news. We move blueberries to our mouths. We play games that involve a dinosaur behind me. I turn to see, and the dinosaur is gone! As is one more blueberry that somehow is hiding behind her mischievous little grin.

The blueberry lesson is baked into my being. I preach it incessantly to the teams I manage and the new leaders I mentor. In my circle of people, those who have joined me on my crazy bus, you will often hear someone say, "Well, blueberry the shit out of that thing!"

Invariably, these people are facing a problem they don't understand. They are applying several rules in succession. And at the end, "Blueberry the shit out of that!"

Tear it apart. Look inside. How does it work? How is it supposed to work? Suddenly lessons 4, 13, and 15 are in full stride, and problems are being solved. The good reader may look behind or ahead as needed, or when reminders are required.

The way I define success in my life and in my career intersect through many of these rules. But the blueberry rule remains at the top of my favorite lessons, as well as my most favorite food.

I still don't know what color a German blueberry is, but I crave that knowledge. I need to call Kim and thank her. I may make her pay double for this book, and double again if she wants my signature because, hey, Lesson 1. But hopefully, she reads this and understands the incredible impact she had on my life.

If you ask her about this, the whole blueberry interaction, maybe she will remember it. Probably, she will say, "Is that jackass still kicking around? I need to call him." And maybe she will.

When I answer, she might say, "Somebody said you wrote some shit about me. I will kick your ass if you told lies! Or if you said anything about those four Welsh guys at the bar!"

And like Han Solo said to Princess Leia in Empire Strikes Back, I will reply, "I know..."

And in my head, I'll finish with, "...that I can still outrun you as long as we're not on that damn boat of yours!"

But by whatever cheese is holey to you, following this rule will filter out so much noise and help you see with so much clarity, you'll want to thank Kim, too. It's a great lesson.

What More Can I Do For You Lesson: Filtering with a service leadership mindset.

"Servant leadership is all about making the goals clear and then rolling your sleeves up and doing whatever it takes to help people win. In that situation, they don't work for you; you work for them."

-Ken Blanchard, Author and business consultant, and this author's favorite business book author

"Service trumps everything else. Great service erases bad experiences. Great service is what we do between the open and close of a service request."

-Kev

For those who have worked with me long enough, they will recognize one of my hallmark habits. At the end of my meetings, and at the conclusion of any phone call, I always ask, "Is there anything more I can do for you?"

This is particularly powerful in contact center situations. The offer is disarming when unexpected and tremendously valuable when actively practiced and executed upon.

Some associates have warned me that the customer's answer can be something well outside your wheelhouse. Do not be deterred! Whatever happens after you have posed this question, if all things are equal, you will have created a lingering positive memory of the interaction.

In a worst-case scenario, the person or people with whom you are talking will open Pandora's Box. And you will always handle every situation as if you needed this extra work. Why? Because you have now made yourself invaluable. You are the person who is happy to help. And most of the time, as you sort out the mess of Pandora's spaghetti requests (think bowl of spaghetti), likely you will merely become a switchboard operator cloaked in the purest shimmering samite while angels vocalize heavenly tunes and people imagine a halo around your head. Your personal mythology grows!

What is really behind this, though? Why is it powerful? Why is it a lesson or a rule found in this book? My answer is that the concept is rooted in "servant leadership" concepts. I am sad if you wonder what servant leadership is. Everybody should know this, and every leader should embrace the philosophy.

So what is "servant leadership?" Conceptually, it's probably how you want your own manager to be. That's not clear enough, though, and there are still many who wish to have Death and his[14] sickle hanging over their shoulder. Still, it's probably how you want your own manager to be. I know I wrote it twice. The Death and sickle folks need to get with the program.

Probably the most commonly seen manifestation defining servant leadership is that old trope of "Boss vs Leader". Most of us have seen it. If you haven't, you're really missing out on something special. But let's look back on this chapter's opening quote by Ken Blanchard.

"Servant leadership is all about making the goals clear and then rolling your sleeves up and doing whatever it takes to help people win. In that situation, they don't work for you; you work for them."

We easily infer from this succinct definition that if your team knows the game plan and you are working side-by-side with them, clearing hurdles, they will succeed.

---

[14] I debated using non-binary language here. There are plenty of examples of both men and women who are shitty managers. But I'll be honest with you: As long as women are not paid equally for the same job, I'm going to assert that the corporate Death character is an arsehole and a man. Thus, "his sickle." Don't like that? Campaign to level compensation to be agnostic of any gender or gender identity. Everybody gets paid for the same base job. Full stop. And then we will be one step closer to "gender" falling in to the only three legitimate buckets: scientific codification, something in your doctor's private files, and nunya.

Really, it's that simple.

Since this book is built upon my ability to tell stories, anecdotes, and leverage random cinematic moments to make my point, I'm going to do that right now. I pepper a few things here, then together, we will identify commonalities.

One cinematic example of a bad manager, or a manager who demonstrates bad leadership principles, is Wanted, a 2008 action film that is a reasonably entertaining film. Bonus points if you think James McAvoy is just brilliant in whatever he does. And McAvoy is the star who, at the beginning of the film, works under a tyrannical manager named Janice. Frankly, I think we've all worked for Janice at one point or another.

Janice constantly uses her position to bully McAvoy's Wesley Gibson, an account manager. [15] Here are some Janice-isms:

"Jesus H. Fuckin' Popsicle! I still don't have my billing reports, but you've got time to sit there and Google your ass off? Well, I know one thing: you've got your review coming up next week, and I can't wait to start checking me off some

---

15 In the film, McAvoy explains that he used to be an Account Service Representative, but a decision was made to manage clients instead of servicing them. This is a grand example of something that comes out of old-school management instead of servant leadership.

big fucking boxes!"

"Attitude, poor. Performance, poor. Management skills, poor. Works well with others? Ha! That's a fucking joke."

"Oh my fucking god! I hope that's not my billing report sitting on your desk. Holy shit on an altar, it is!"

It pains me to think of this. Yet here is what we have from Janice.

Janice starts off using hostile profanity as she yells at Wesley for not giving her the outcome she wanted. She follows that with a threat to alter or adjust his upcoming review. Drop another f-bomb in there, and Janice doubles down on her threat. [16]

The second quote is just insults and some sad sarcasm. That's a fine bit of bullying, to boot. All of this done in front of Wesley Gibson's peers.

The final quote gives us more profanity, a measure of outcomes, and more sarcasm to bully Wesley in front of the team.

---

[16] Don't get me wrong. I'm a potty mouth of epic proportions. An expertly presented F-bomb in a sentence is like using just the right amount of salt and pepper when preparing your most favorite steak. There's a difference, however, between "f-ing" and "f you". The former is for impressively emphasizing or illustrating your point. The latter is a typically unacceptable personal attack. But the former can be used abusively. Janice uses it abusively, in a hostile manner. No part of leadership or teamwork involves hostility.

Janice gives me the cringes. Is it a justifiable act to respond as Wesley finally does? Asking for a friend. Send your responses to me through certified, insured, overnight mail in the form of a jelly donut for no, or a random key from a standard off-white keyboard for yes.

So, while Wesley may have known the goal, the reports, he didn't have the support of a servant leader. He had an abusive, hostile bully. Wesley failed for many reasons. Plot aside, most of those reasons were Janice. Let's move on.

Another cinematic example of this kind of manager is Darth Vader from the original three movies. Yes, Darth Vader. Arguably the greatest villain of all time, but a bad manager. Here are some examples of Vader's bad management style:

"Don't be too proud of this technological terror you've constructed. The ability to destroy a planet, or even a whole system, is insignificant next to the power of the Force."

"I find your lack of faith disturbing."

"Where are those transmissions you intercepted? What have you done with those plans? If this is a consular ship, where is the ambassador?"

"You don't know the power of the dark side! I must obey my master."

"I am altering the deal. Pray I don't alter it any further."

"When I left you, I was but the learner. Now I am the master."

And this is all from the first film that was actually the fourth in the series. Let's do a quick analysis of Vader's management style.

The first quote marginalizes the work his team had done. He compares their output (which is admittedly a marvel unto itself) to his own capabilities.

The second quote belittles a team member for not believing in Vader's religion. It comes along with the frightening implication of "disturbing. [17]"

The third quote is all about Vader asking rhetorical questions, then punishing the team member with the life-ending, lifted-physically-off-the-ground choke. It seems a bit on the unfair side of things, really. At least let the guy put in a word edgewise.

---

17 Spoiler alerts and stuff. Frankly, this is my most favorite of Vader's quotes. Until Rogue One came along, there never was a forthright example demonstrating why Vader was a feared and powerful Sith Lord. It was all a mythology masterfully implied through writing, screenplay, directing, etc. And then even with dueling Luke, allegedly torturing Leia, and blocking a blaster shot by Han Solo, everything terrifying and evil about Vader was inferred by you, the watcher. And then Rogue One gifted us with seeing this savage, rage-filled servant of evil. After that, the Disney+® series titled Obi-Wan Kenobi gave us even more of a taste of bad Vader.

The fourth and fifth quotes fall in the same bucket. They are authoritarian, absolute, and absent anybody's input. Vader would have made a great Borg. "I must obey my master! Resistance is futile! You will be assimilated." How many readers just threw this book against the wall? How many of those readers were sitting on the toilet whilst reading this book? This could go pear-shaped real fast.[18]

The final quote is a near-exact characteristic of those managers we want to avoid. Essentially, Vader sought rank. For those who watched the first three episodes, Anakin Skywalker, the larval stage of Darth Vader, demonstrated all too often how he was upset for not being moved from the rank of padawan to that of Jedi, or for not being made a Master when they added him to the Jedi Council, or even in his own mind for how he viewed the pecking order between himself and Obi-Wan Kenobi. It was all about rank, title, position. He didn't want to earn it through harsh, refining, character-building lessons, or through pure merit. Anakin just made it all about rank.

As much as I love this character, or the Darth Vader part of it, he is a walking, talking, midichlorian- packed master class of how

---

[18] If you are offended by my mixing of science fiction and science fantasy characters or entities, that is not a me problem. That is a you problem. My words, my book. Read or read not. That passed the grammar checker. Yoda was a genius.

not to lead, unless fear, bullying, and cold-blooded murder is your thing. Not one single person in the Empire's employ worked for a servant leader. It was abuse and bullying, threats and violence, bad dialog and a great story. Once again, they knew the goal and were pushed beyond the brink, ala Elon Musk and his Twitter team pre-layoffs. No support from leadership at all. [19]

Now let us look at two examples of actual servant leadership. I'll continue with cinematic examples. However, I could name a very small handful of actual people I know who fit that bill.[20]

My go-to for just about everything is Mary Poppins. In the

---

[19] Note that I am not disparaging Musk here. That human is genius as an engineer and as an entrepreneur. I merely contend that entrepreneurs do not operate well in reality in the sense that they might understand what they've asked their teams to deliver, or what it takes to get there. I was once forced to make a team of developers work 90-hour work weeks three weeks in a row to deliver something our President wouldn't review until it was too late in the game to be realistic about her new demands. It was hideous, and it was driven by one of the greatest entrepreneurs I have ever met. She flushed more great ideas down the toilet each morning than most people have in their entire lives. That level of genius lived by "demand, not understand." I'll carry the guilt of not doing better for that team for the rest of my days.

[20] They know who they are, I hope, and I wouldn't want to overtly link them to this particular effort without first asking their permission. That would kind of ruin things for me "Hey, I think you're awesome and I'm writing a book. Can I mention your name?" Just, no. Remember: my words, my book. I'm sure someone, or a lot of someones, will not like this or will take offense to what or how I write. Nobody should be seen in a lesser light because of my words and actions. So to those of you who know who you are, thanks. I'm thinking of you.

context of this chapter, Mary Poppins may just be the single greatest servant leader in cinematic history. Here are some examples of servant leadership behaviors we see in the English nanny, followed by characteristics Mary Poppins demonstrated and how they line up with Ken Blanchard's definitions.

In the "spoonful of sugar" scene, Poppins sets a goal of cleaning a bedroom for Michael and Jane. Then she starts in by explaining to the children that "...in every job that must be done, there is an element of fun. You find the fun and...Snap! The job's a game!" She proceeds to sing, walk about the room, and closes an open drawer, stands up a rocking horse, and basically leading by example as she shows the children that she will clean along with them.

Service leadership at its best right there. And while there are underlying social and familial commentaries throughout the movie, everything Poppins does for the Banks family is to help them improve their lives, their relationships, and their own selves.

Go watch Mary Poppins again. Not for entertainment, but to learn. With your learning hat on, the movie takes on a whole new meaning.

Next, I want to lean on Uncle Buck for servant leadership examples. Yes, the John Candy movie. Yes, Uncle Buck.

Uncle Buck is a lazy, non-committal underachiever. He gambles, he won't work for his girlfriend's tire shop, and he doesn't hold jobs. But when Uncle Buck is asked to watch his nieces and nephew, he steps up.

The older niece and oldest of the children, Tia, is difficult and overplays the rebellious teenage angsty girl. Uncle Buck sets the game plan and his expectations. Despite her repeated efforts to sabotage him, some being tragically successful, Uncle Buck sticks with the game plan, continues to support her, and comes to her rescue toward the end of the movie.

Uncle Buck tries to help Tia be successful through the entire movie. He never deviates. He sees through her struggles to understand who she really is. And in the end, he helps her fix her relationship with her parents, but not until his exquisite vengeance on Bug, the predatory this-is-the-guy-your-parents-warned-you-about guy who is trying to get Tia to sleep with him. Everybody needs an Uncle Buck at home or at work. Everybody.

To wrap up the chapter, it is important to understand why this is here, in a book about filters. I enjoy using movies to demonstrate what I'm trying to teach. People understand this. And I'm using these examples to further aid in filtering out the noise and distractions. We're here to solve problems.

If we are not constantly engaging with our peers, customers, team members, etc., to help solve problems, noise arises. I firmly believe every reader just nodded their head. The noise arises when complacency, boredom, a lack of challenges starts creeping in.

To prevent that noise, drive people around you to raise up the problems requiring solutions. Focus on that, and the noise stays out of the way. It's a filter caused by driving the conversation, trying to help, and always asking what else you can help with. Always.[21]

---

[21] Ever since I watched Harry Potter and the Deathly Hallows II, where Potter is using the pensieve to see Severus Snape's memories, I cannot use the word "always" without thinking of Alan Rickman's genius skills. Nothing to do with this book. Rickman's Snape was genius acting from the first movie to the last.

The Finish Line Lesson:

Life's Dichotomy Paradox

"There is no spoon."

-That one bald monk kid in The Matrix

"Zeno of Elia. That guy warps reality with impossible truths."

-Kev, a guy who otherwise doesn't believe in the impossible

Zeno of Elia is my favorite philosopher. As I point out in the quote above, he kind of warps reality. Case in point: Zeno's dichotomy paradox.

In the event that you are not familiar with Zeno and the dichotomy paradox, I'll briefly explain.

Zeno's dichotomy paradox posits that given two points of time, X and Y, an object in motion cannot reach its destination. Why? Because to reach the destination, the object must first reach the halfway point. And to reach the halfway point, the object must first reach the halfway point to the halfway point. And to reach that point, ad nauseum. And since there are an infinite number of halfway points between here and there, that object can never reach its destination.

Sure, that makes sense...as much as it reeks of cow patty. By the old gods, the new gods, and everything in between, I love philosophy!

This is where it reminds me of the other quote in this chapter. Think back to when you first watched The Matrix and Neo met the bald monk kid in the Oracle's apartment. The kid is bending his spoon with his mind but goes on to explain to Neo that there is no spoon. Sure, but we're all looking at him holding a bendy spoon. OK.

Like I said, I love philosophy!

So, what does that have to do with filters and this book? Is there any irony in the fact that this is the Finish Line and the final chapter? Sure.

The truth of the matter is that with this kind of stuff, we have to remember the words of that one bald monk kid holding his spoon that isn't really there. Indeed, there is no spoon.

There is no finish line. There is no end to this. Even when we master the way our filters work, we cannot slip into complacency. Make your filter noise proof and someone will build louder noise. Isn't that what they say?

I don't know. Maybe sayings aren't my thing. But it took a lot of effort to get to this point, to refine the rules and lessons, and they have evolved over the years. There has been learnings and input and revisions and support from so many people. In fact, the stories have evolved over about 20 years or so and people have been asking for a book for about the same amount of time.

My hope is that even just one paragraph of one chapter resonates with you. At least one. The folks who have worked with me through the years have truly benefitted from this content, grown with it, found joy and success with it, and in some cases even moved on to even better roles using these lessons.

I hope the same for every reader.

Remember, there is no finish line. With every word you read, with every lesson you learn and apply, each is just one more brick you add to your own personal building of who you will become up until you take your last breath.

And hopefully, you can leave your own book or books behind, your own legacy for your teams, your children, or whomever may be important to you. Your words and thoughts have value. Share them. Destroy the finish line. Keep the race going.

May your filters always help you find peace and joy!

About the Author

Kevin Carly was born in San Pablo, California and early in life moved to Utah. He was raised under the gaze of the majestic Wasatch mountains until he rebelled against rejection from the Navy's ROTC program.

This created the opportunity for a medical discharge from the United States Army about a year and a half after graduating from American Fork High School.

Kevin spent some time without a sail or rudder while working in the restaurant industry before, as he likes to say, Forrest Gumping his way into a long career in technology.

Having worked for some of the largest names in their vertical markets, Kevin found great success in IT Operations, Project Management, and his real love, Contact Centers, where he has done a great deal of "hired gun" activity.

Kevin has been involved in mining and energy, advertising and marketing, automotive retail software, ERP, organizational change management consulting, contact center creation and repair consulting, network engineering, messaging platform consulting, and more.

He holds over 30 technical certifications, a BS in Information Systems, an MBA in MIS, a SCP Certified Support Manager, and recently he acquired certifications in OCI Foundations and OCI AI Foundations because he asked his team to do the same. Kevin is a HUGE fan of Oracle technologies. He is currently randomly working on the OCI Networking Professional certification course. Just because he can.

For hobbies, Kevin loves basketball, is a life-long <Insert City Here> Raiders football fan and loves basketball in general. He enjoys failing at 3D and resin printing. Kevin loves horses and spreadsheets (the latter because he can be the most boring human on the planet.)

Kevin became an Dudeist priest in 2016. He also loves debating politics, religion, philosophy, and believes that in another life he failed to be an epidemiologist there, too.

Throughout his life, Kevin has lived in Utah, Illinois, and Michigan. Always, the call of Utah brings him home to his family. Kevin seems to be better off as a single man, having been married to two different women. He has four of his own children and a couple more from other people procreating. These children collectively brought into the world 6.5 grandchildren as of January 2024. Most of these humans live within 15 minutes of Kevin's Springville, Utah, home.

This makes Kevin feel he is an amazingly fortunate human. He abides.

9 798348 217600